Triangles and Beyond

BRITANNICA
Mathematics in Context

Geometry and Measurement

TEACHER'S GUIDE

HOLT, RINEHART AND WINSTON

Mathematics in Context is a comprehensive curriculum for the middle grades.
It was developed in 1991 through 1997 in collaboration with the Wisconsin Center
for Education Research, School of Education, University of Wisconsin-Madison and
the Freudenthal Institute at the University of Utrecht, The Netherlands, with the
support of the National Science Foundation Grant No. 9054928.

The revision of the curriculum was carried out in 2003 through 2005, with the
support of the National Science Foundation Grant No. ESI 0137414.

National Science Foundation

Opinions expressed are those of the authors
and not necessarily those of the Foundation.

Roodhardt, A., de Jong, J. A., Abels, M., de Lange, J., Brinker, L. J., Middleton, J. A.,
Simon, A. N., and Pligge, M. A. (2006). *Triangles and beyond.* In Wisconsin Center
for Education Research & Freudenthal Institute (Eds.), *Mathematics in context.*
Chicago: Encyclopædia Britannica, Inc.

The Teacher's Guide for this unit was prepared by David C. Webb, Elaine McGrath,
and Mieke Abels.

ISBN 0-03-039814-2

5 6   073   09 08 07

The *Mathematics in Context* Development Team

Development 1991–1997

The initial version of *Triangles and Beyond* was developed by Anton Roodhardt and Jan Auke de Jong.
It was adapted for use in American schools by Laura J. Brinker, James A. Middleton, and Aaron N. Simon.

Wisconsin Center for Education

Research Staff

Thomas A. Romberg
Director

Joan Daniels Pedro
Assistant to the Director

Gail Burrill
Coordinator

Margaret R. Meyer
Coordinator

Project Staff

Jonathan Brendefur
Laura Brinker
James Browne
Jack Burrill
Rose Byrd
Peter Christiansen
Barbara Clarke
Doug Clarke
Beth R. Cole
Fae Dremock
Mary Ann Fix

Sherian Foster
James A, Middleton
Jasmina Milinkovic
Margaret A. Pligge
Mary C. Shafer
Julia A. Shew
Aaron N. Simon
Marvin Smith
Stephanie Z. Smith
Mary S. Spence

Freudenthal Institute Staff

Jan de Lange
Director

Els Feijs
Coordinator

Martin van Reeuwijk
Coordinator

Mieke Abels
Nina Boswinkel
Frans van Galen
Koeno Gravemeijer
Marja van den Heuvel-Panhuizen
Jan Auke de Jong
Vincent Jonker
Ronald Keijzer
Martin Kindt

Jansie Niehaus
Nanda Querelle
Anton Roodhardt
Leen Streefland
Adri Treffers
Monica Wijers
Astrid de Wild

Revision 2003–2005

The revised version of *Triangles and Beyond* was developed by Mieke Abels and Jan de Lange.
It was adapted for use in American Schools by Margaret A. Pligge.

Wisconsin Center for Education

Research Staff

Thomas A. Romberg
Director

David C. Webb
Coordinator

Gail Burrill
Editorial Coordinator

Margaret A. Pligge
Editorial Coordinator

Project Staff

Sarah Ailts
Beth R. Cole
Erin Hazlett
Teri Hedges
Karen Hoiberg
Carrie Johnson
Jean Krusi
Elaine McGrath

Margaret R. Meyer
Anne Park
Bryna Rappaport
Kathleen A. Steele
Ana C. Stephens
Candace Ulmer
Jill Vettrus

Freudenthal Institute Staff

Jan de Lange
Director

Truus Dekker
Coordinator

Mieke Abels
Content Coordinator

Monica Wijers
Content Coordinator

Arthur Bakker
Peter Boon
Els Feijs
Dédé de Haan
Martin Kindt

Nathalie Kuijpers
Huub Nilwik
Sonia Palha
Nanda Querelle
Martin van Reeuwijk

Cover photo credits: (all) © Getty Images; (middle) © Kaz Chiba/ PhotoDisc

Illustrations
x (left) Map from the Road Atlas © 1994 by Rand McNally; (right) © Encyclopædia Britannica, Inc.; **xviii** (all), **5** Christine McCabe/ © Encyclopædia Britannica, Inc.; **8** © Encyclopædia Britannica, Inc.; **10, 25** Christine McCabe/© Encyclopædia Britannica, Inc.; **29** Holly Cooper-Olds; **45, 48** (top), **49** Christine McCabe/© Encyclopædia Britannica, Inc.; **55** Holly Cooper-Olds

Photographs
x Historic Urban Plans, Inc.; **xvii** © Corbis; xviii Victoria Smith/HRW; **1** (top left, and bottom) © Corbis; (top right) © Arthur S. Aubry/PhotoDisc/Getty Images; **2** Iain Davidson Photographic/Alamy; **3, 4** © Corbis; **5** copyrighted by Amish Country Quilts "Amish Country Quilts, Lancaster, PA—www.amish-country-quilts.com"; **11** Victoria Smith/HRW; **47** Courtesy of Michigan State University Museum; **49** Victoria Smith/HRW; **51** © PhotoDisc/Getty Images

Contents

Dear Teacher,

Welcome! *Mathematics in Context* is designed to reflect the National Council of Teachers of Mathematics *Principles and Standards for School Mathematics* and the results of decades of classroom-based education research. *Mathematics in Context* was designed according to the principles of Realistic Mathematics Education, a Dutch approach to mathematics teaching and learning. In this approach mathematical content is grounded in a variety of realistic contexts in order to promote student engagement and understanding of mathematics. The term *realistic* is meant to convey the idea that the contexts and mathematics can be made "real in your mind." Rather than relying on you to explain and demonstrate generalized definitions, rules, or algorithms, students investigate questions directly related to a particular context and develop mathematical understanding and meaning from that context.

The curriculum encompasses nine units per grade level. *Triangles and Beyond* is designed to be the fourth unit in the Geometry and Measurement Strand, but the unit also lends itself to independent use—to introduce students to the geometric properties of triangles and other polygons such as parallelograms.

In addition to the Teacher's Guides and Student Books, *Mathematics in Context* offers the following components that will inform and support your teaching:

- *Teacher Implementation Guide,* **which provides an overview of the complete system and resources for program implementation.**

- *Number Tools* **and** *Algebra Tools,* **which are black-line master resources that serve as review sheets or practice pages to support the development of basic skills and extend student understanding of concepts developed in number and algebra units.**

- *Mathematics in Context Online,* **which is a rich, balanced resource for teachers, students, and parents looking for additional information, activities, tools, and support to further students' mathematical understanding and achievements.**

Thank you for choosing *Mathematics in Context.* We wish you success and inspiration!

Sincerely,

The Mathematics in Context Development Team

Triangles and Beyond and the NCTM Principles and Standards for School Mathematics for Grades 6-8

The process standards of Problem Solving, Reasoning and Proof, Communication, Connections, and Representation are addressed across all *Mathematics in Context* units.

In addition, this unit specifically addresses the following PSSM content standards and expectations:

Number and Operations

In grades 6–8 all students should:

* understand and use the inverse relationships of squaring and finding square roots to solve problems.

Algebra

In grades 6–8 all students should:

* represent, analyze, and generalize a variety of patterns with tables, words, and when possible, symbolic rules.

Geometry

In grades 6–8 all students should:

* precisely describe, classify, and understand relationships among types of two- and three-dimensional objects using their defining properties;
* create and critique inductive and deductive arguments concerning geometric ideas and relationships, such as congruence, similarity, and the Pythagorean relationship;
* describe sizes, positions, and orientations of shapes under informal transformations such as flips, turns, slides, and scaling;
* examine the congruence, similarity, and line or rotational symmetry of objects using transformations;
* draw geometric objects with specified properties, such as side lengths or angle measures;
* use geometric models to represent and explain numerical and algebraic relationships; and
* recognize and apply geometric ideas and relationships in areas outside the mathematics classroom, such as art, science, and everyday life.

Measurement

In grades 6–8 all students should:

* select and apply techniques and tools to accurately find length, area, and angle measures to appropriate levels of precision

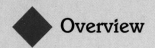
Math in the Unit

Prior Knowledge

This unit assumes that students are able to identify a triangle, measure lengths using a centimeter ruler, and measure angles with a protractor or compass card. Students should be familiar with properties of regular polygons and should know that there are 180° in a semicircle or straight angle.

From the unit *Facts and Factors,* students should be familiar with square numbers. In addition, it will be helpful if students are able to use a compass to draw a circle.

In *Triangles and Beyond,* a unit in the substrand Shapes and Construction, students develop a more formal understanding of the properties of triangles. Students also develop a more formal understanding of *parallel* and define *parallelogram, rectangle, rhombus,* and *square* in their own words.

Triangles

After identifying triangles in their surroundings, students try to make triangles with various sets of three sticks of different lengths. Students learn to construct triangles given the length of the sides using a pair of compasses.

Classification of Triangles

Students will classify triangles according to their side length: *equilateral, isosceles,* and *scalene triangles,* and according to their angles: *right, acute,* and *obtuse triangle.*

Properties of Triangles

Students investigate several general properties of triangles:

The sum of the lengths of any two sides must be greater than the length of the third side. This property is named the Triangle Inequality theorem, but students do not have to know this name.

The longest side of a triangle is opposite the largest angle, which is known as the Opposite Parts theorem, or Hinge theorem, but students do not have to know this name.

$$AB + BC > AC$$
$$AB + AC > BC$$
$$AC + BC > AB$$

In several situations, students explore the relationship of the angles of a triangle: The sum of the angles of a triangle is 180°.

On the Road to the Pythagorean Theorem

When students make triangles using squares, they discover that a right triangle is formed only when the sum of the areas of the two smaller squares equals the area of the largest square.

When the area of the largest square is less than the sum of the sum of the areas of the two smaller squares, then the triangle is an acute triangle. When the area of the largest square is more than the sum of the sum of the areas of the two smaller squares, then the triangle is an obtuse triangle. (See sample picture. 16 > 9 + 4.)

Students use this relationship at an informal level, which can be described at a formal level as follows.

If a is the longest side of a triangle, and the other two sides are b and c, then the three sides of an obtuse triangle have the relationship $a^2 + b^2 < c^2$ and the three sides of an acute triangle have the relationship $a^2 + b^2 > c^2$.

The Pythagorean Theorem

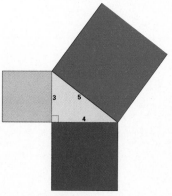

If a triangle has a right angle, then the square on the longest side has the same area as the other two squares combined.

In this unit, the Pythagorean theorem is not formally stated as $a^2 + b^2 = c^2$, but is presented using area language. To help students develop insight into the possible application of this theorem, use area language frequently. Students should understand that this theorem applies only to right triangles.

Parallel lines

The properties of parallel lines are investigated and introduced:

- they are always the same distance apart;
- they never touch;
- they form equal angles with a line that intersects them. (The name for this intersecting line is *transversal;* students do not have to know this name here.)

Students will use these properties when they investigate parallelograms.

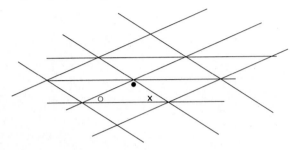

The concept of *families of parallel lines* is introduced and used:

- to "proof" the property of the angles of a triangle: the sum of the angles is 180º.
- to start an investigation of the properties of congruent triangles, which is continued in the eighth grade unit *It's All the Same,* where students investigate the properties of congruent and similar triangles.

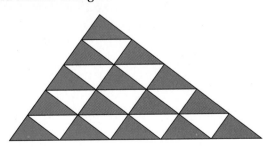

Translations

Given definitions for the terms *congruent*, *translation*, *rotation*, and *reflection*, students use animal stamps and their own designs to gain informal experience with these concepts. Translations are combined to construct regular polygons, parallelograms, and rectangles.

Notations

In this unit the following notations are introduced:

The angle symbol, ⌐, to designate right angles

The symbol △ for the word *triangle*, so triangle *ABC* can be replaced by △ *ABC.*

When students have finished the unit they will:

- recognize and classify: triangles (equilateral, isosceles, and scalene triangles; right, acute, and obtuse triangles) and quadrilaterals (parallelogram, rectangle, rhombus, and square);
- have developed the concept of parallel lines, the Pythagorean theorem, congruent figures, line of symmetry, and transformations (translations, rotations, and reflections);
- make constructions of triangles given the side lengths and of parallel lines and families of parallel lines; and
- use the properties of triangles and parallel lines to solve problems with the Pythagorean theorem and the rule that the sum of the angle measurements in a triangle is 180°.

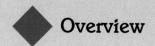

Geometry and Measurement Strand: An Overview

In the MiC units, measurement concepts and skills are not treated as a separate strand. Many measurement topics are closely related to what students learn in geometry. The geometry and measurement units contain topics such as similarity, congruency, perimeter, area, and volume. The identification of and application with a variety of shapes, both two-dimensional and three dimensional, is also addressed.

The developmental principles behind geometry in *Mathematics in Context* are drawn from Hans Freudenthal's idea of "grasping space." Throughout the strand, ideas of geometry and measurement are explored. Geometry includes movement and space—not just the study of shapes. The major goals for this strand are to develop students' ability to describe what is seen from different perspectives and to use principles of orientation and navigation to find their way from one place to another.

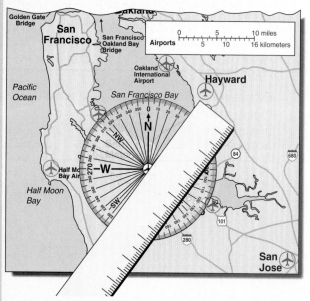

The emphasis on spatial sense is related to how most people actually use geometry. The development of students' spatial sense allows them to solve problems in the real world, such as identifying a car's blind spots, figuring out how much material to buy for a project, deciding whether a roof or ramp is too steep, and finding the height or length of something that cannot be measured directly, such as a tree or a building.

Mathematical content

In *Mathematics in Context*, geometry is firmly anchored in the physical world. The problem contexts involve space and action, and students represent these physical relationships mathematically.

Throughout the curriculum, students discover relationships between shapes and develop the ability to explain and use geometry in the real world. By the end of the curriculum, students work more formally with such geometric concepts as parallelism, congruence, and similarity, and use traditional methods of notation as well.

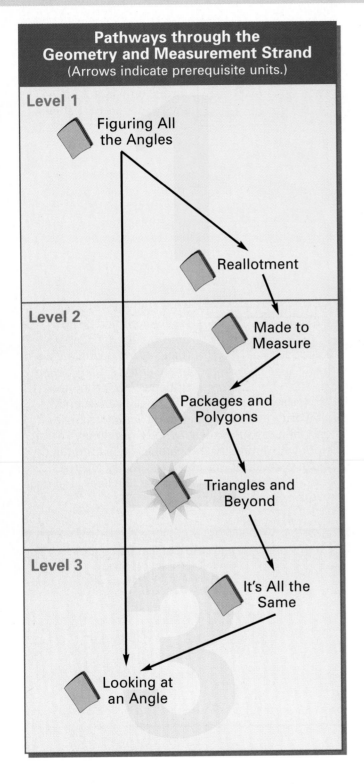

**Pathways through the
Geometry and Measurement Strand**
(Arrows indicate prerequisite units.)

Level 1

Figuring All
the Angles

Reallotment

Level 2

Made to
Measure

Packages and
Polygons

Triangles and
Beyond

Level 3

It's All the
Same

Looking at
an Angle

Organization of the Geometry and Measurement Strand

Visualization and representation is a pervasive theme in the Geometry strand and is developed in all of the Geometry and Measurement strand units. The units are organized into two substrands: Orientation and Navigation, and Shape and Construction. The development of measurement skills and concepts overlaps these two substrands and is also integrated throughout other *Mathematics in Context* units in Number, Algebra, and Data Analysis.

Orientation and Navigation

The Orientation and Navigation substrand is introduced in *Figuring All the Angles*, in which students are introduced to the cardinal, or compass, directions and deal with the problems that arise when people in different positions describe a location with directions. Students use maps and compass headings to identify the positions of airplanes. They look at angles as turns, or changes in direction, as well as the track made by a sled in the snow. They discern different types of angles and learn formal notations and terms: vertex, $\angle A$, and so on. The rule for the sum of the angles in a triangle is informally introduced. To find angle measurements students use instruments such as a protractor and compass card.

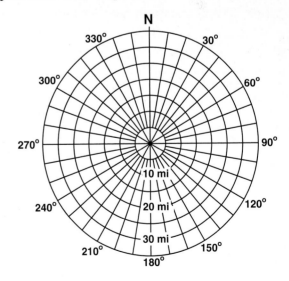

In *Looking at an Angle*, the last unit in the Geometry strand, the tangent ratio is informally introduced. The steepness of a vision line, the sun's rays, a ladder, and the flight path of a hang glider can all be modeled by a right triangle. Considering the glide ratio of hang gliders leads to formalization of the tangent ratio. Two other ratios between the sides of a right triangle are introduced, the sine and the cosine. This leads to formalization of the use of the Pythagorean theorem and its converse.

Shape and Construction

Reallotment is the first unit in the Shape and Construction substrand. Students measure and calculate the perimeters and areas of quadrilaterals, circles, triangles, and irregular polygons. Students learn and use relations between units of measurement within the Customary system and the Metric System.

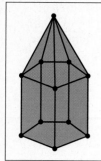

Does Euler's formula work for a five-sided tower? Explain your answer.

Solids are introduced in *Packages and Polygons*. Students compare polyhedra with their respective nets, use bar models to understand the concept of rigidity, and use Euler's formula to formally investigate the relationships among the numbers of faces, vertices, and edges of polyhedra.

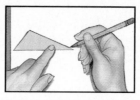

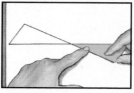

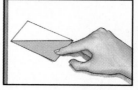

In *Triangles and Beyond*, students develop a more formal understanding of the properties of triangles, which they use to construct triangles. The concepts of parallel lines, congruence, and transformation are introduced, and students investigate the properties of parallel lines and parallelograms. A preformal introduction to the Pythagorean theorem is presented.

After studying this unit, students should be able to recognize and classify triangles and quadrilaterals. In the unit *It's All the Same*, students develop an understanding of congruency, similarity, and the properties of similar triangles and then use these ideas to solve problems. Their work with similarity and parallelism leads them to make generalizations about the angles formed when a transversal intersects parallel lines, and the Pythagorean theorem is formalized.

If a triangle has a right angle, then the square on the longest side has the same area as the other two combined.

Measurement

The concept of a measurement system, standardized units, and their application overlaps the substrands of Orientation and Navigation, and Shape and Construction. Furthermore, the development and application of measurement skills is integrated throughout units in the Number, Algebra, and Data Analysis strands, through topics such as use of ratio and proportion, finding and applying scale factors, and solving problems involving rates (for instance, distance-velocity-time relationships).

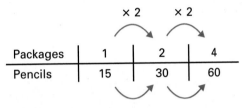

		×2	×2
Packages	1	2	4
Pencils	15	30	60

In *Mathematics in Context*, the Metric System is used not only as a measurement system, but also as a model to promote understanding of decimal numbers.

The unit *Made to Measure* is a thematic measurement unit where students work with standard and non-standard units to understand the systems and processes of measurement. They begin by studying historic units of measure such as foot, pace, and fathom (the length of outstretched arms). Students use their own measurements in activities about length, area, volume, and angle and then examine why standardized units are necessary for each.

The relationships between measurement units are embedded in the number unit, *Models You Can Count On*, where students explore conversions between measures of length within the Metric System. The measurement of area in both metric and Customary Systems is explicitly addressed in the unit *Reallotment*. Students also learn some simple relationships between metric and customary measurement units, such as 1 kilogram is about 2.2 pounds, and other general conversion rules to support estimations across different measurement systems. In *Reallotment, Made to Measure,* and *Packages and Polygons*, the concepts of volume and surface area are developed. Strategies that were applied to find area measurements in *Reallotment* are used to derive formulas for finding the volume of a cylinder, pyramid, and cone.

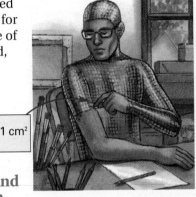

1 cm²

Visualization and Representation

Visualization and representation is a component of every geometry unit. In *Mathematics in Context*, this theme refers to exploring figures from different perspectives and then communicating about their appearance or characteristics.

In *Reallotment*, students use visualizations and representations to find the areas of geometric figures. They decide how to reshape geometric figures and group smaller units into larger, easy-to-count units. They also visualize and represent the results for changing the dimensions of a solid. In the unit *It's All the Same*, students visualize triangles to solve problems.

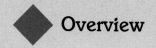
Student Assessment in Mathematics in Context

As recommended by the NCTM *Principles and Standards for School Mathematics* and research on student learning, classroom assessment should be based on evidence drawn from several sources. An assessment plan for a *Mathematics in Context* unit may draw from the following overlapping sources:

- **observation—As students work individually or in groups, watch for evidence of their understanding of the mathematics.**

- **interactive responses—Listen closely to how students respond to your questions and to the responses of other students.**

- **products—Look for clarity and quality of thought in students' solutions to problems completed in class, homework, extensions, projects, quizzes, and tests.**

Assessment Pyramid

When designing a comprehensive assessment program, the assessment tasks used should be distributed across the following three dimensions: mathematics content, levels of reasoning, and difficulty level. The Assessment Pyramid, based on Jan de Lange's theory of assessment, is a model used to suggest how items should be distributed across these three dimensions. Over time, assessment questions should "fill" the pyramid.

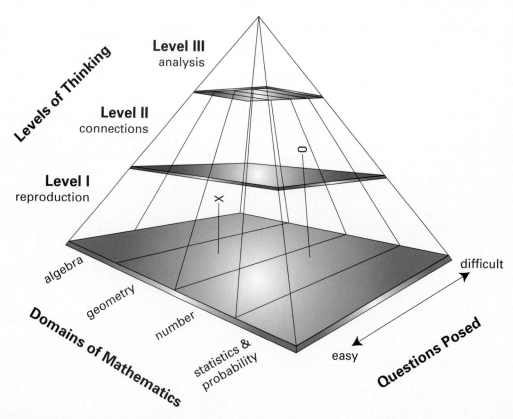

Levels of Reasoning

Level I questions typically address:

- recall of facts and definitions and
- use of technical skills, tools, and standard algorithms.

As shown in the pyramid, Level I questions are not necessarily easy. For example, Level I questions may involve complicated computation problems. In general, Level I questions assess basic knowledge and procedures that may have been emphasized during instruction. The format for this type of question is usually short answer, fill-in, or multiple choice. On a quiz or test, Level I questions closely resemble questions that are regularly found in a given unit substituted with different numbers and/or contexts.

Level II questions require students to:

- integrate information;
- decide which mathematical models or tools to use for a given situation; and
- solve unfamiliar problems in a context, based on the mathematical content of the unit.

Level II questions are typically written to elicit short or extended responses. Students choose their own strategies, use a variety of mathematical models, and explain how they solved a problem.

Level III questions require students to:

- make their own assumptions to solve open-ended problems;
- analyze, interpret, synthesize, reflect; and
- develop one's own strategies or mathematical models.

Level III questions are always open-ended problems. Often, more than one answer is possible, and there is a wide variation in reasoning and explanations. There are limitations to the type of Level III problems that students can be reasonably expected to respond to on time-restricted tests.

The instructional decisions a teacher makes as he or she progresses through a unit may influence the level of reasoning required to solve problems. If a method of problem solving required to solve a Level III problem is repeatedly emphasized during instruction, the level of reasoning required to solve a Level II or III problem may be reduced to recall knowledge, or Level I reasoning. A student who does not master a specific algorithm during a unit but solves a problem correctly using his or her own invented strategy may demonstrate higher-level reasoning than a student who memorizes and applies an algorithm.

The "volume" represented by each level of the Assessment Pyramid serves as a guideline for the distribution of problems and use of score points over the three reasoning levels.

These assessment design principles are used throughout *Mathematics in Context.* The Goals and Assessment charts that highlight ongoing assessment opportunities—on pages xvi and xvii of each Teacher's Guide—are organized according to levels of reasoning.

In the Lesson Notes section of the Teacher's Guide, ongoing assessment opportunities are also shown in the Assessment Pyramid icon located at the bottom of the Notes column.

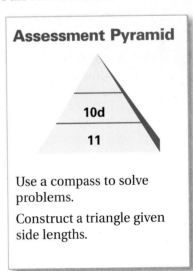

Assessment Pyramid

10d

11

Use a compass to solve problems.

Construct a triangle given side lengths.

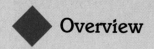
Goals and Assessment

In the *Mathematics in Context* curriculum, unit goals organized according to levels of reasoning described in the Assessment Pyramid on page xiv, relate to the strand goals and the NCTM *Principles and Standards for School Mathematics*. The *Mathematics in Context* curriculum is designed to help students demonstrate their understanding of mathematics in each of the categories listed below. Ongoing assessment opportunities are also indicated on their respective pages throughout the Teacher's Guide by an Assessment Pyramid icon.

It is important to note that the attainment of goals in one category is not a prerequisite to the attainment of those in another category. In fact, students should progress simultaneously toward several goals in different categories. The Goals and Assessment table is designed to support preparation of an assessment plan.

	Goal	Ongoing Assessment Opportunities	Unit Assessment Opportunities
Level I: Conceptual and Procedural Knowledge	**1.** Use propeties of triangles (e.g., sum of angles, side relationships, the Hinge theorem, and the Pythagorean theorem.	**Section C** p. 19, #8e p. 21, #15c **Section D** p. 24, #2ab p. 31, #16ab	**Quiz 1** #3b **Quiz 2** #2 **Test** #1cd, 4, 5acd
	2. Construct a triangle given side lengths.	**Section B** p. 13, #11	**Quiz 1** #2 **Quiz 2** #1
	3. Construct and identify (families of) parallel lines.	**Section A** p. 5, #11ab **Section F** p. 45, #4a	**Quiz 1** #1ab **Test** #3a
	4. Recognize and classify triangles.	**Section B** p. 10, #2 **Section D** p. 24, #2a p. 27, #6, 7	**Quiz 1** #3a **Quiz 2** #1 **Test** #2, 3b, 5d
	5. Recognize and classify quadrilaterals.	**Section F** p. 46, #7	**Test** #3a
	6. Understand and identify line symmetry.	**Section E** p. 39, #8abc	**Quiz 2** #3abc

	Goal	Ongoing Assessment Opportunities	Unit Assessment Opportunities
Level II: **Reasoning,** **Communicating,** **Thinking,** **and Making** **Connections**	7. Describe geometric figures using words and diagrams.	**Section C** p. 18, #7ab p. 20, #13 **Section D** p. 24, #2c **Section F** p. 47, #9	**Test** #3a
	8. Describe transformations (translation, rotation, and reflection) using words and diagrams	**Section E** p. 38, #5 **Section F** p. 49, #11, 12	**Quiz 2** #3bc **Test** #1ab
	9. Use a compass to demonstrate and solve problems	**Section B** p. 12, #8d p. 13, #10d	**Quiz 1** #2
	10. Describe angle relationships that occur when one line intersects one or more lines.	**Section C** p. 16, #1a **Section F** p. 45, #3ef	

	Goal	Ongoing Assessment Opportunities	Unit Assessment Opportunities
Level III: **Modeling,** **Generalizing,** **and Non-Routine,** **Problem Solving**	11. Develop general statements for geometric relationships	**Section A** p. 4, #7c, 8 **Section B** p. 9, #1b **Section C** p. 16, #1b p. 17, #3, 4 p. 20, #10b **Section D** p. 28, #11b	**Test** #5b
	12. Use counterexamples to justify geometric properties.	**Section A** p. 7, For Further Reflection **Section F** p. 50, #13e	

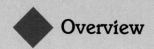
Materials Preparation

The following items are the necessary materials and resources to be used by the teacher and students throughout the unit. For further details, see the Section Overviews and the Materials section of the Hints and Comments column of each teacher page. Note: Some contexts and problems can be enhanced through the use of optional materials. These optional materials are listed in the corresponding Hints and Comments section.

Student Resources

Quantities listed are per student.
- **Letter to the Family**
- **Student Activity Sheets 1–10**

Teacher Resources

Quantities listed are per class.
- Newspapers and magazines, several

Student Materials

Quantities listed are per pair of students, unless otherwise noted.
- **Blank transparency**
- **Calculator (one per student)**
- **Centimeter grid paper**
- **Centimeter ruler (one per student)**
- **Colored pencils, one box**
- **Colored pens (3 different colors)**
- **Compass (one per student)**
- **Drawing paper (nine sheets per student)**
- **One large white paper (poster-size)**
- **Pictures of triangles gathered by students on page 2**
- **Plastic or cardboard triangle**
- **Protractor or compass card**
- **Scissors**
- **Sets of spaghetti pieces, made by students on page 8**
- **Straightedge or ruler**
- **String (about 1 to 2 meters)**
- **Tape**
- **Thick paper (or index cards)**
- **Toothpicks (12)**
- **Tracing paper**
- **Uncooked spaghetti, four strands**

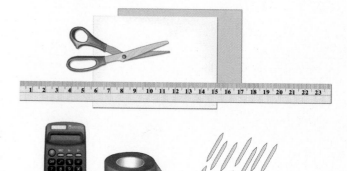

BRITANNICA
Mathematics in Context

Student Material and Teaching Notes

◆ Contents

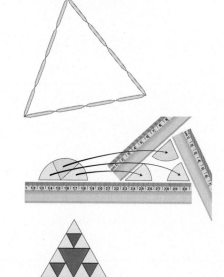

Dear Student,

Welcome to *Triangles and Beyond.*

Pythagoras, a famous mathematician, scientist, and philosopher, lived in Greece about 2,500 years ago. Pythagoras described a way of constructing right angles. In this unit, you will learn about the Pythagorean theorem and how you can use this theorem to find the length of sides of right triangles.

In this unit, there are many investigations of triangles and quadrilaterals and their special geometric properties.

You will study the properties of parallel lines and learn the differences between parallelograms, rectangles, rhombuses, and squares.

As you study this unit, look around you to see how the geometric shapes and properties you are studying appear in everyday objects. Does the shape of a picture change when you change its orientation on the wall from vertical to horizontal? How are parallel lines constructed? This unit will help you understand the properties of shapes of objects.

Sincerely,

The Mathematics in Context Development Team

Section Focus

In this section students start to investigate the two topics that play an important role in the entire unit: triangles and (families of) parallel lines. Students identify triangles in two- and three-dimensional situations in pictures and in the world around them. They investigate and describe the differences between lines that are parallel and lines that are not parallel. Three properties of parallel lines are formalized. At the end of this section, students identify families of parallel lines and investigate the triangular grid that families of parallel lines can make. The instructional focus of Section A is to:

- **identify triangles in various diagrams and pictures;**
- **investigate how perspective affects the shape of a triangle; and**
- **solve problems involving parallel lines.**

Pacing and Planning

Day 1: Triangles Everywhere		Student pages 1–3
INTRODUCTION	Problem 1	Identify triangles in the classroom and in a set of pictures.
CLASSWORK	Problems 2–5	Identify triangles in diagrams and explore the effect of perspective on the shape of a triangle.
HOMEWORK	Activity, page 2	Make a poster out of triangular objects from newspapers and magazines.

Day 2: Side by Side		Student pages 3–7
INTRODUCTION	Problems 6–8	Identify and describe parallel and non-parallel lines.
CLASSWORK	Problems 9–13	Solve problems involving parallel lines and angles formed by lines that intersect parallel lines.
HOMEWORK	Problem 14; Check Your Work For Further Reflection	Student self-assessment: Identify triangles and describe the relationship between parallel lines and angles.

Additional Resources: Additional Practice Section A, page 54.

Materials

Student Resources
Quantities listed are per student.

- Letter to the Family
- Student Activity Sheet 1

Teachers Resources
Quantities listed are per class.

- Newspapers and magazines, several

Student Materials
Quantities listed are per pair of students, unless otherwise noted.

- Colored pens (3 different colors)
- Drawing paper (one per student)
- Grid paper (one per student)
- Straightedge or ruler
- Toothpicks (12)

* See Hints and Comments for optional materials.

Learning Lines

Parallel Lines

This section introduces the properties of parallel lines:

- they are always the same distance apart;
- they never touch;
- they form equal angles with a line that intersects them (The name for this intersecting line is *transversal*; students do not have to know this name here).

Students will use these properties in Section F, where they investigate parallelograms.

Families of Parallel Lines

In Section C, families of parallel lines are used to "proof" the property of the angles of a triangle: the sum of the angles is 180°.

In the unit *It's All the Same*, students investigate the properties of congruent and similar triangles, using a triangular grid that is made by three families of parallel lines.

Representation, Spatial Abilities

Students explore three dimensional drawings; they draw side views and front views; and they will be aware that actual shapes of objects can not always be seen in a three dimensional drawing because of the perspective.

At the End of This Section

Students have further developed their spatial abilities. They have developed their understanding of the concept of parallel lines and families of parallel lines. They know properties of parallel lines. They can find equal angles when a line intersects two parallel lines.

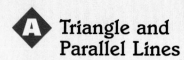
Notes

Discuss properties of triangles—what they have in common, what makes some special. You will get feedback on students' prior knowledge.

Triangles and Parallel Lines

Triangles Everywhere

Look around your classroom and find several triangles.

1. Make a list of all the triangles you can find in these pictures.

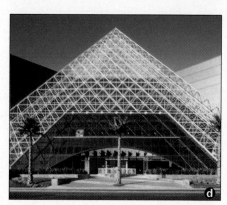

Solutions and Samples

1. Descriptions may vary. Sample responses:

   Triangles can be seen in the sails, the kite, the bridge, the building.

Hints and Comments

Materials

triangular objects or pictures of triangles (optional, several per class);
newspapers and magazines (optional, several per class)

Overview

Students identify triangles in pictures.

Planning

You could start this section with a whole class discussion. Ask students to make a list of all the triangles they see in the classroom.

Comments About the Solutions

If the classroom does not contain many triangles, ask, *What other common objects have parts that are shaped like triangles?* Sample responses: protractor, gables or windows on houses, spokes on wheels, pieces in kaleidoscopes, faces of pyramids, road sign, triangles formed by a diagonal bar at the back of a bookcase (to stabilize an open bookcase).

Some students may identify objects that have an implied triangular shape, such as the two hands of a clock.

You may remind the students of the stable structures they studied in the unit *Packages and Polygons*. This would be a nice introduction to the context on the next page: an iron bridge.

1. Students may work on problem 1 individually. When they are done, you may want to take a class inventory and discuss their answers.

Bringing Math Home

You might have students look for triangles at home or in other places. They may involve their families in their search for triangles.

Notes

Have students save their work for the activity because they will need to use it later in the unit.

2 This problem is an opportunity to develop students' ability to draw side views of objects that are shown in a perspective drawing.

You may want to point out that even though the Big Dipper and other constellations are seen as ``flat'' or two dimensional, the stars in those constellations are millions of miles away from each other.

3 You may want to point out the difference between triangles where the beams touch and triangles that are seen even though the beams do not touch.

Finding Triangles

Find some other examples of triangular objects in pictures from magazines and newspapers. Paste the pictures in your notebook or make a poster or a collage. Save your examples. You will need to use these examples of triangular objects throughout this unit.

Here is a photograph of a bridge over the Rio Grande River near Santa Fe, New Mexico. The construction of iron beams forms many triangles. Different viewing perspectives change the appearance of the triangles.

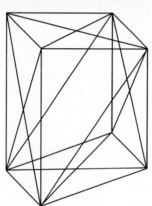

Here is a drawing of one section of the bridge.

2. **a.** Draw a side view of this section.

   b. How many triangles can you find in your side view?

3. In this section of the bridge, how many triangles do the iron beams form? You may want to make a three-dimensional model to help you answer the question.

Reaching All Learners

Hands-On Learning

If students have difficulty visualizing the triangles in the bridge's frame, you might have them construct a model using toothpicks and clay or gumdrops. You could also have them use a model that is available in the classroom. If you have students create a model using a net, have them fold it together and indicate the beams with a marker.

Vocabulary Building

In a class discussion you could review the term *face diagonal* from the unit *Packages and Polygons*.

Solutions and Samples

2. a. There are several different side views that could be drawn. One example:

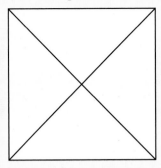

b. 8 triangles:

 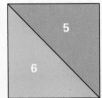 

3. 40 triangles

If students come up with 36 triangles, they may have reasoned in the following way: In four side views, you have 4 × 8 = 32 triangles, and in the other two side views, you have 2 × 2 = 4 triangles. So, together 32 + 4 = 36 triangles. This is correct, but the students have overlooked four other triangles. The rods between three vertices (they are all face diagonals), as shown below, also form triangles. There are four such triangles.

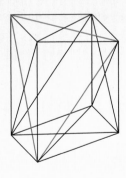 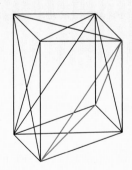

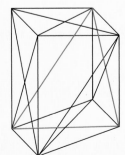 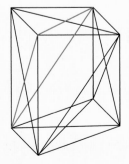

Hints and Comments

Materials

newspapers and magazines (several per class); toothpicks, optional (20 per student); clay or gumdrops, optional (10 pieces per student); copies of a net of a cube; scissors, tape, markers, optional (one of each per student)

Overview

Students find pictures of triangles in magazines or newspapers. They then paste the pictures in their notebooks or make a poster with them.

They draw a side view and identify triangles.

About the Mathematics

Students learned to recognize, draw, and reason about different views of objects in the unit *Packages and Polygons*.

Planning

The Activity can be assigned as homework. Students may work on problems 2 and 3 individually. Discuss students' answers in class.

Some students need a concrete model of the section of the bridge. It can be very time consuming if they make it by themselves in class. In order to avoid that, you could make one large model in advance and have it available in class.

Comments About the Solutions

Activity

You may want to have students make a collage or use notebooks to keep track of their collections.

A Triangle and Parallel Lines

Notes

4a Students should discuss the different triangles they see.

4b Students may want to visualize what the house would look like from the other side.

This might be a good opportunity for students to share their experiences with drawing perspective and vision lines.

6 Ask students to find other examples of lines in the classroom that share this special property. Edges of bulletin boards, window frames, and lines on a tile floor are other examples of parallel lines.

Some houses have slanted roofs, like this. Slanted roofs form interesting triangles.

4. a. Count the number of triangles you can find in the drawing of the house.

b. Do you think there are any triangles on the house that you cannot see in the drawing? Explain.

Sometimes you cannot see the actual shapes of the triangles and other objects in a drawing because of the perspective of the drawing.

5. a. Sketch the front view of the house. Pay attention to the shape of the triangular gable, the pitched roof above the front door.

b. Why does the shape of the front triangle on the gable differ from your drawing?

Side by Side

6. What is special about the lines in this photograph?

Reaching All Learners

Accommodation

It may be helpful for some students to have a copy of this page so they can outline the triangles on the house with a marker.

English Language Learners

Gable may be a new word for some ELL students. A gable is the triangular end of a sloped roof.

Solutions and Samples

4. a. There are six triangles visible, as shown in the drawing below:

b. Yes. There must be at least one other triangle for the other peak of the roof.

5. a. Drawings will vary. Sample drawing:

b. Answers will vary. Sample student response:

The side lengths and the angle measurements in the two triangles are different because the sketch in the book is drawn at an angle, while my drawing is from directly in front of the house.

6. Answers will vary, but these lines are (roughly) parallel. Sample student responses:

They are straight lines.
They run alongside one another.
The lines never touch.
The lines all run in the same direction.

Hints and Comments

Materials

drawing paper (one sheet per group of students); transparency (optional, one per class); overhead projector (optional, one per class); colored overhead pens (optional, two colors per class); other pictures of houses (optional, one per student)

Overview

Students identify triangles that can be seen in the drawing of a house and reason about triangles that cannot be seen. They also investigate distortion due to perspective. Students start to investigate parallel lines.

About the Mathematics

Students investigated faces that were "hidden" in the unit *Packages and Polygons.*

Parallel lines in a two-dimensional picture may have a vanishing point. Students should realize that although the lines seem to come closer to one another in the picture, they are parallel in reality.

Planning

Students may work on problem 4 in small groups. Problems 5 and 6 can be done individually.

Comments About the Solutions

6. Allow students to use their own words to describe the lines in the photograph. Some students may notice that the field is harvested and that the distance between the rows is the same. Other students may think that the rows get closer to each other at the end of the field. If so, explain that the rows only appear to get closer.

Extension

You may wish to have students bring in other pictures of houses. Then discuss how drawings or photographs may distort the actual dimensions of a house.
You might have students experiment with visualizing distorted figures by drawing shapes on a transparency, projecting them on the overhead, and having students look at the screen from different places in the room. You can also hold the transparency at an angle to the overhead.

A Triangle and Parallel Lines

Notes

7b Discuss how to find the shortest distance between the lines.

To create a right angle for getting the shortest distance, an index card works well. Have students draw the perpendicular lines that they are measuring.

7c Coloring the two angles helps students identify exactly what they are measuring.

Here is an aerial view of another field. The lines in the field are parallel. The word **parallel** comes from a Greek word meaning *side by side*.

7. a. On **Student Activity Sheet 1**, select two parallel lines in the diagram and trace them using a colored pencil or marker.

b. Measure how far apart the two lines are at several points. What do you notice?

c. Measure the angles between the two lines and the road. What can you conclude?

8. Draw two lines that are *not* parallel. Describe two ways that you recognize lines that are not parallel.

This is the National Aquarium in Baltimore, Maryland. The building has a very unusual roof structure. Within each triangular face, there are several families of parallel lines. A **family of parallel lines** is a set of lines that are all parallel to one another.

9. a. On **Student Activity Sheet 1**, choose one triangular face. How many families of parallel lines can you find on that face?

b. Highlight each family of parallel lines with a different color.

Parallel lines do not intersect (cross); they are always the same distance apart. Parallel lines form equal angles with lines that intersect them.

Here are three parallel lines and one line that intersects them. Some angles that are equal are marked with the same symbol.

10. a. Copy this drawing in your notebook and mark all equal angles with the same symbol.

b. **Reflect** Measure the angle sizes to verify your work. Describe any relationships among the angles.

Assessment Pyramid

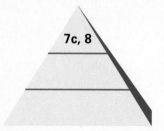

7c, 8

Develop general statements for geometric relationships.

Reaching All Learners

Accommodation

Some students will find it helpful to have the drawing reproduced on an index card so they can cut out an angle and slide it along to check for equal angles.

Extension

You may want to ask students to look for pictures or drawings of buildings and roads in newspapers. Then ask students to indicate parallel lines or families of parallel lines in their pictures. You may display their results in your classroom.

Solutions and Samples

7. a. Note that students may have colored different pair of parallel lines.

b. Answers will vary. Sample responses:

They are an equal distance apart everywhere (0.8 cm, or 8 mm).

c. The angles they make with the road are equal (about 118 degrees measured from the right-hand side, or 62 degrees measured from the left-hand side).

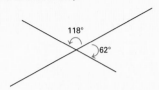

8. Drawings will vary. Sample answers:

Lines are not parallel if they intersect. Lines are not parallel if they make different angles with a third line that intersects them.

9. a. There are two families of parallel lines on the side facing the reader: one family of lines runs vertically, and the other family of lines runs horizontally.

b.

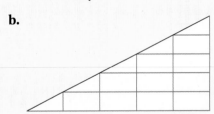

10. a.

b. Descriptions may vary. Students may notice that only two different symbols are used, or in other words: there are only two different sized angles in the drawing.

Students may see that an angle marked with a red × and an angle marked with a blue circle form a semicircle, or are together 180°.

Hints and Comments

Materials

compass card or protractor and straightedge (one per student); transparent paper (optional, one sheet per student); **Student Activity Sheet 1** (one per student); colored pencils (one box per group); pictures or drawings of buildings from newspapers or magazines, (optional, several per student)

Overview

Students investigate some characteristics of parallel lines. They identify families of parallel lines, and they use symbols to indicate equal sized angles.

About the Mathematics

This page introduces the properties of parallel lines:

- they are always the same distance apart;
- they never touch;
- they form equal angles with a line that intersects them. (The name for this intersecting line is *transversal*; students do not have to know this name here.)

Students will use these properties in Section F, where they investigate parallelograms.

Planning

Students may work on these problems in small groups. You may want to discuss problem 7 with the whole class.

Comments About the Solutions

7. c. Students may measure the angles with a compass card or protractor and compare the measurements. Another way to compare the angles is to use transparent paper. Students can trace one angle and put it on the other angles in order to see whether it fits.

9. Student Activity Sheet 1 is also used for problem 12 on the next page.

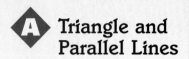

A Triangle and Parallel Lines

Notes

Here is a part of a patchwork quilt.

11. a. How many families of parallel lines do you recognize?

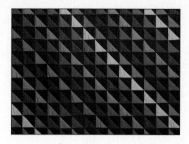

b. Copy the pattern on grid paper and use colored markers to indicate the families of parallel lines. Use a different color for each family.

Here is a part of the face of the roof of the National Aquarium. The intersections of the two families of parallel lines can be used to create a third family. The slanted side of the roof is a member of this family.

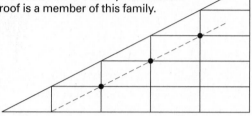

12. a. Use **Student Activity Sheet 1** to draw all the lines in the third family.

b. Is this third family really a family of parallel lines? Why or why not?

c. The result of your drawing is a triangular grid. Color the triangles in the grid to make a pattern. Choose any pattern you wish.

13 This problem takes some time to do; it is a good one to have students do at home so they do not feel rushed. If students are struggling, you could ask what is special about the quadrilaterals and how this might affect the kind of triangles they are making.

13. Here is an arrangement made of 12 toothpicks. Rearrange any four toothpicks to create exactly six triangles.

14. Reflect Compare the triangular grids from problems 11, 12, and 13.

a. Which arrangements do you like the most? Why?

b. What are the similarities and differences among the triangles in these arrangements?

Assessment Pyramid

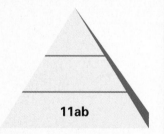

11ab

Construct and identify families of parallel lines.

Reaching All Learners

Extension

Challenge students to create their own toothpick puzzle.

Parent Involvement

You might have students involve their families in their search for a solution of problem 13.

Solutions and Samples

11. a. Three families of parallel lines.

   b. Sample response:

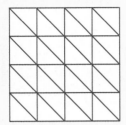

12. a.

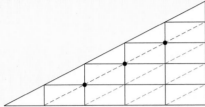

   b. Yes, because the lines of this third family do not intersect.

   c. Students may color different patterns.

     Sample pattern:

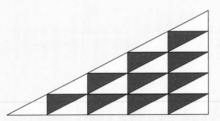

13. Move the colored toothpicks. Sample solution:

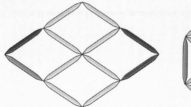

14. a. Answers may vary, Sample response: I like the one in problem 13 the most because it is more regular.

   b. Answers may vary. Sample responses:
A similarity is that each pattern exists out of one type of triangle.

     A difference is that a triangle in problem 11 is half of a square, while a triangle in problem 12 is half of a rectangle.

     A triangle in problem 11 has two equal sides. The sides of a triangle in problem 12 are all different. A triangle in problem 13 has equal sides.

Hints and Comments

Materials

Students Activity Sheet 1 (one per student); grid paper (one piece per student); toothpicks (12 per pair of students); colored markers (3 different colors)

Overview

Students draw families of parallel lines. They compare the different triangular grids that three families of parallel lines can make.

About the Mathematics

The triangles that are formed by three families of parallel lines are congruent. The concept of congruency is introduced in Section E.

Planning

Students may work on these problems in pairs. You may want to discuss problem 14b with the whole class.

Notes

The Summary formalizes the ideas from the section. Discuss memory hooks for the word *parallel*. For example, the "double L" in the word should trigger an image of parallel lines. Also have them model parallel lines with two pencils or their arms.

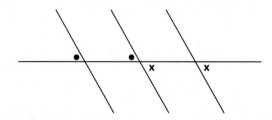

Triangles appear in many places. Some triangles are part of a building structure; some others are part of the pattern in artwork.

Parallel lines do not intersect.

Parallel lines are always the same distance apart.

Parallel lines form several equal angles with lines that intersect them.

Families of parallel lines create interesting patterns.

Check Your Work

A logo for an organization is pictured here.

1. How many families of parallel lines can you find in this logo?

Here is a logo for another organization.

2. How many triangles can you find in this logo?

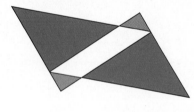

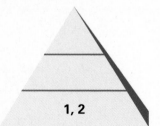

1, 2

Assesses Section A Goals

Reaching All Learners

Parent Involvement

Have students reread the Summary with their parents. Students can share the angle patterns that appear with families of parallel lines. Which angles appear to be equal? Which angle pairs form a straight line?

Accommodation

Some students may find it helpful to have a copy of the logo so they can use a separate color for each family of parallel lines and write on it when they are counting the triangles. Making each triangle a separate color aids in counting.

Solutions and Samples

Answers to Check Your Work

1. Two families are visible: one around COMCO and the second at the outer edges of the triangles.

2. There are six triangles in total: two large interlocking triangles, two small triangles at opposite corners, and two medium triangles in the other corners.

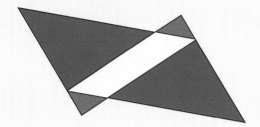

Hints and Comments

Materials

A copy of the logo (optional)

Overview

Students read the Summary, which formalizes the main concepts of this section.

Check Your Work Problems

These problems are designed for student self-assessment. A student who can answer the questions correctly has understood enough of the concepts taught in the section to be able to start the next section. Students who have difficulties in answering the questions without help may need extra practice. This section is also useful for parents who want to help their children with their work.

Answers are provided in the Student Book. Have students discuss their answers with classmates.

About the Mathematics

Some teachers may want to point out that the pair of angles marked with an o and an x in the Summary diagram have a special name: they are called corresponding angles.

Whenever two or more parallel lines are crossed by a third line, corresponding angles are found on the same side of the parallel lines and the line that intersects them. Names of other special angle pairs are discussed in the Hints and Comments on the next page.

Comments About the Solutions

2. If students have difficulty finding triangles in the logo, then problem 3 on Student Book page 54 can be used as extra practice. Note that they need a copy of **Student Activity Sheet 9** to do this problem.

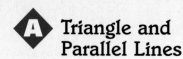

Triangle and Parallel Lines

Notes

Have students share their approach for finding equal angles. There are various ways to mark angle pairs, and it is important for students to hear different approaches.

3 Any students having difficulty with finding the congruent angles could cut out the angle with the dot and use it as a measuring tool.

For Further Reflection

Reflective questions are meant to summarize and discuss important concepts

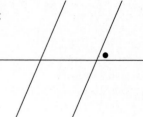

This picture shows two parallel lines crossed by a third line. There is a dot in one of the angles formed by the intersecting lines.

3. **a.** Copy the picture into your notebook. Use a dot to designate all angles that are equal in measure to the angle shown.

   b. Describe the relationships among the angles that do *not* have dots.

 ## For Further Reflection

Can you make a triangle that has two sides that are parallel? Use a drawing to explain your answer.

Assessment Pyramid

FFR

3

Assesses Section A Goals

Reaching All Learners

Advanced Learners

This problem suggests the use of a counter example to justify an impossible figure. You might refer students to a property of triangles (where all three sides must intersect) to justify why it cannot be drawn using parallel lines (which never meet).

Accommodation

Having straws, popsicle sticks, or toothpicks available might be helpful for exploring the question posed in For Further Reflection.

Solutions and Samples

3. a.

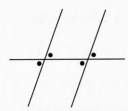

b. All the angles in the drawing that do not have a dot are equal to one another.

For Further Reflection

Sample response:

In my drawing on the left you see that two sides are parallel because they make the same angle of 90° with the base of the triangle. But the picture will not become a triangle because the two sides that go up will never meet. In the drawing on the right you see that the vertical lines make different angles with the base, so they will meet somewhere.

Hints and Comments

Materials

Straws, popsicle stick, toothpicks (optional)

Planning

After students complete Section A, you may assign appropriate activities from the Additional Practice section, located on page 54 of the Triangles and Beyond Student Book, as homework.

About the Mathematics

After students complete problem 3, some teachers may want to point out the special names of two other types of equal angle pairs: vertical angles and alternate interior angles.

Whenever two lines intersect, the angles that are opposite from each other are called vertical angles (marked v).

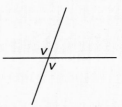

Whenever two parallel lines are crossed by a third line, the angle pair on opposite sides of the third line and in between the parallel lines are called alternate interior angles (marked Alt Int).

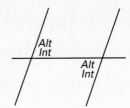

Section Focus

Students try to make triangles with various sets of three sticks of different lengths and discover a generalization: the sum of the lengths of any two sides must be greater than the length of the third side. Students start to classify triangles according their side lengths: equilateral, isosceles, and scalene triangles. At the end of the section, students learn to construct triangles given side length using a pair of compasses. The instructional focus of Section B is to:

- **investigate and apply the geometric property that the two shorter sides of a triangle are always longer than the longest side;**
- **identify equilateral, isosceles, and scalene triangles; and**
- **Construct a triangle given the length of its sides.**

Pacing and Planning

Day 3: Making Triangles		Student pages 8–10
ACTIVITIES	Problems 1 and 5	Investigate the properties of triangles by constructing triangles using pieces of spaghetti and toothpicks.
HOMEWORK	Problems 2–4	Identify equilateral, isosceles, and scalene triangles.

Day 4: Looking at the Sides		Student pages 11 and 12
INTRODUCTION	Problem 6	Sketch a scale drawing of a triangle.
CLASSWORK	Problems 7 and 8	Construct a triangle given the lengths of its three sides.
HOMEWORK	Problem 9	Apply the properties of triangles to solve problems.

Day 5: Looking at the Sides (continued)		Student pages 12–15
INTRODUCTION	Review homework	Review homework from Day 4.
CLASSWORK	Problems 10 and 11	Construct a triangle given the lengths of its three sides.
HOMEWORK	Check Your Work; For Further Reflection	Student self-assessment: Construct a triangle from three given sides.

Additional Resources: Additional Practice Section B, pages 54–56

Materials

Student Resources
Quantities listed are per student.

- Student Activity Sheet 2

Teachers Resources
No resources required.

Student Materials
Quantities listed are per pair of students, unless otherwise noted.

- Centimeter ruler
- Compass (one per student)
- Pictures of triangles gathered by students on page 2
- Sets of spaghetti pieces, made by students on page 7
- String (about 1 to 2 meters)
- Uncooked spaghetti, four strands

* See Hints and Comments for optional materials.

Learning Lines

Properties of Triangles

When students have tried to construct triangles given side length, they described in their own words the requirements for the side length. This is described more formally in the Summary.

For a triangle, the sum of the lengths of any two sides is greater than the length of the remaining side.

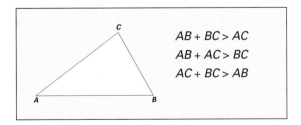

$$AB + BC > AC$$
$$AB + AC > BC$$
$$AC + BC > AB$$

Classification of Triangles

In this section, students classify triangles according their side lengths (equilateral, isosceles, and scalene triangles). In Section D, students classify triangles according the measurements of the angles.

Constructions

To draw a point at a certain distance from point *A* can be done using a centimeter ruler. Students will review that a pair of compasses is the best tool to use when they have to find all locations that are at a certain distance from point *A*. This understanding is essential in order to be able to construct a triangle given side lengths.

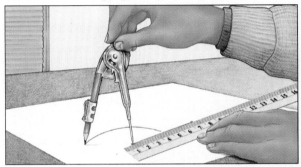

At the End of This Section

Students can recognize and classify equilateral, isosceles, and scalene triangles.

They can explain whether or not a triangle can be constructed using the given side lengths. They start to learn how to use a pair of compasses for constructions.

The Sides

B

Activity

Making Triangles

For this activity, you need four long pieces of uncooked, dry spaghetti.

- Carefully break one piece of spaghetti into the lengths shown for set A.
- Break the others to match the lengths for sets B, C, and D.

Note: The pieces of spaghetti are not to scale.

Note that the lengths of the spaghetti pieces shown on this page are not actual sizes.

Students have to use a centimeter ruler to break the pieces of spaghetti into their correct lengths.

Set A		Set B	
3 cm		3 cm	
4 cm		3 cm	
5 cm		7 cm	

Set C		Set D	
3 cm		3 cm	
5 cm		4 cm	
7 cm		7 cm	

1a To save class time, you may want to have a copy of the chart available for students. Encourage students to sketch the results of their trials.

1. **a.** Try to make a triangle with the three lengths in each set. Copy and complete the chart to summarize your work.

	Sides (in cm)	Sketch of What Happened	Can You Make a Triangle? Explain.
Set A	3, 4, 5		
Set B	3, 3, 7		
Set C	3, 5, 7		
Set D	3, 4, 7		

Reaching All Learners

Accommodation

Spaghetti works well, but narrow strips of paper or drinking straws could be substituted for the spaghetti. If paper is used, the lengths can be recorded on each strip. The spaghetti or strips should be stored in an envelope or plastic baggie for use again on page 9.

Solutions and Samples

1. a. Sketches and explanations will vary. Sample table:

	Sides (in cm)	Sketch of What Happened	Can You Make a Triangle? Explain.
Set A	3, 4, 5		Yes.
Set B	3, 3, 7		No, the sides didn't reach.
Set C	3, 5, 7		Yes.
Set D	3, 4, 7		No, the triangle was flat.

Hints and Comments

Materials

uncooked, dry spaghetti (four strands per student); crayons or markers (optional, three colors per student); centimeter ruler (one per student); copies of the sets on a transparency (optional, one per student)

Overview

Students break pieces of spaghetti to match lengths that are given. They will use these sets of spaghetti strands to make triangles.

Planning

Students may begin the activity individually. Each student should make each set of spaghetti lengths. You may wish to have students color the tips of the pieces of spaghetti in each set a different color. Save the sets of spaghetti strands for use later in this section.

Students may complete problem 1a individually before discussing problems 1b and 1c on page 9 in small groups.

B The Sides

Notes

1b Some students may need to investigate more combinations. If necessary, ask some questions to help them discover the requirement. For example, ask, *Why does set B not work? Would 2, 3, 7 work?*

1c Some students may need a reminder of what a 90° angle looks like. Have them model with two pencils what an angle larger than 90° and an angle smaller than 90° look like.

Activity

Classifying Triangles
Students could work together on this, trying to make all possible triangles and to classify them. You may want to ask students if all equilateral triangles are also isosceles and if all isosceles triangles are also equilateral. A Venn diagram might help explain this.

b. Reflect In order to form a triangle, there is a requirement for the lengths of the three sides. Describe this requirement in your own words.

c. Describe the angles of each triangle that you were able to make.

Triangles are classified into three categories according to the lengths of their sides. Note that sides with the same length are marked with the same number of slashes.

- Triangles with three equal sides are called **equilateral triangles**.

- Triangles with at least two equal sides are called **isosceles triangles**.

- Triangles with three sides of different lengths are called **scalene triangles**.

Classifying Triangles

Use all of the pieces of spaghetti from the previous activity to make several equilateral, isosceles, and scalene triangles. Sketch each triangle in your notebook. Measure and record the side lengths of each triangle. Classify each triangle according to the lengths of the sides.

Assessment Pyramid

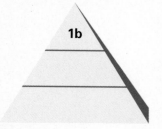

Develop general statements for geometric relationships.

Reaching All Learners

Vocabulary Building

Discuss possible memory hooks for the terms *equilateral, isosceles,* and *scalene.* You may want to have students put these words on index cards with the definition and a sketch on the back. Vocabulary posters in the room are also a good idea. The cards can be used for review games at the end of the unit.

Extension

Ask, *Is it possible to draw a triangle that is not scalene, isosceles, or equilateral?* Have students explain why or why not. (No, because these are the only types of triangles that exist.)

Solutions and Samples

1. b. Answers will vary. Sample response:

The sum of any two sides of a triangle must be greater than the length of the third side.

c. Answers will vary. Sample responses:

Set A made a triangle with a right angle and two smaller angles.

Set C had one angle larger than a right angle and two angles smaller than a right angle.

Activity

Possible equilateral triangles:

- 3 cm, 3 cm, 3 cm
- 7 cm, 7 cm, 7 cm

Possible isosceles triangles:

• 3, 3, 3	• 4, 4, 3	• 5, 5, 3	• 7, 7, 3
• 3, 3, 4	• 4, 4, 5	• 5, 5, 4	• 7, 7, 4
• 3, 3, 5	• 4, 4, 7	• 5, 5, 7	• 7, 7, 5
			• 7, 7, 7

Possible scalene triangles:

- 3 cm, 4 cm, 5 cm
- 3 cm, 5 cm, 7 cm
- 4 cm, 5 cm, 7 cm

Hints and Comments

Materials

sets of spaghetti strands, made by students on page 8 of the Student Book (four sets per student)

Overview

Students try to create triangles using the sets of spaghetti pieces they made. They discover a requirement for the lengths of the three sides of a triangle. They also learn the names of different types of triangles, classified according to the lengths of the sides: equilateral, isosceles, and scalene triangles.

About the Mathematics

Given three line segments, the length of any one side must be shorter than the sum of the lengths of the other two sides in order to form a triangle. This property is named the Triangle Inequality theorem, or Hinge theorem, but students do not have to know these names.

Planning

Students may complete problem 1a on page 8 individually before discussing problems 1b and 1c in small groups.

Comments About the Solutions

1. b. Students should discover that a triangle cannot be made out of any three line segments. Instead, the length of any one side must be shorter than the sum of the lengths of the other two sides. Otherwise, the triangle either is flat or cannot be closed at all. You may want to discuss students' answers as a class and formulate a class definition for this rule.

1. c. Some students may remember the concepts of obtuse and acute triangles from *Figuring All the Angles*. These concepts will be reviewed in Section D, where they classify triangles according the size of their largest angle.

B The Sides

B The Sides

Notes

3 You might ask students, *How many isosceles triangles are possible?* (Infinitely many.)

5 Using a straightedge helps get the toothpicks in a straight line.

Looking at the Sides

2. Classify the six triangles you made from toothpicks for problem 13 on page 5.

3. Without using a ruler, create an isosceles triangle by folding a strip of paper or a drinking straw. How can you make certain your triangle is an isosceles triangle? Draw a sketch of it.

4. In Section A, you collected pictures of triangles. Which of your examples are isosceles triangles? Which are equilateral? Which are scalene?

Activity

5. Make all possible triangles from exactly 12 toothpicks. Record your results from the activity in a table like the one shown below.

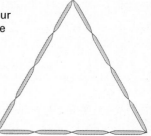

Number of Toothpicks for Side 1	Number of Toothpicks for Side 2	Number of Toothpicks for Side 3	Type of Triangle

Assessment Pyramid

Classify triangles.

Reaching All Learners

Intervention

For problem 5, discuss ways students should organize their table so they do not miss any possibilities.

Connections to Prior Knowledge

This is a good opportunity to review the rule that the sum of any two sides of a triangle must be greater than the third side. You might ask some questions such as: *Why is 1, 2, 9 not on the list of possible triangles, but 2, 6, 6 is on the list?* Try to get students to state the rule. Many of them probably used it when they made their list.

Solutions and Samples

2. They are all equilateral triangles.

3. Any isosceles triangle is acceptable, but students should be able to show how they made two sides equal.

   Students may make an isosceles triangle in two steps. First, they should fold one part of the straw or strip in order to get two pieces of the same length:

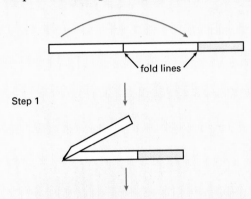

fold lines

Step 1

   Second, students should bend the unequal piece to complete the triangle:

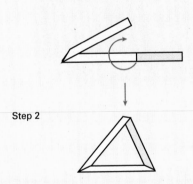

Step 2

4. Answers will vary, but students should be able to justify their answers by showing that isosceles triangles have at least two equal sides; equilateral triangles have three equal sides; and scalene triangles have sides of three different lengths.

Hints and Comments

Materials

straw or strip of paper, optional (one per student); pictures of triangles gathered by students on page 2 of the Student Book (several per student); toothpicks, optional (12 per student)

Overview

Students make different types of triangles from toothpicks and identify them as equilateral, isosceles, or scalene. They record their results in a table.

Planning

Problems 2 and 3 can be done individually or in small groups before students discuss them in class. Problems 4 and 5 may be done individually and used for informal assessment. Problem 5 may also be assigned as homework. Students may work on the activity in small groups

Comments About the Solutions

2. This problem may lead to a discussion about the definitions of isosceles and equilateral triangles. Ask students, *Are all equilateral triangles isosceles? Are all isosceles triangles equilateral?* (Equilateral triangles are also isosceles, but not all isosceles triangles are equilateral.)

5. The only possibilities are mentioned in the table. Note that for example 3–3–6 is not a triangle. You may have to discuss this in class and look back at the Summary of Section A.

Number of Toothpicks for Side 1	Number of Toothpicks for Side 2	Number of Toothpicks for Side 3	Type of Triangle
2	5	5	isosceles
3	4	5	right
4	4	4	equilateral

Notes

6c Students may not be familiar with how to create a scale. If that is the case, you could ask them how many meters 1 cm could represent so the drawing would fit on their paper. Let them struggle for a while to see how difficult it is to construct a triangle with sides lengths that are predetermined. They may come up with some good strategies.

Remind students that they need to use the scale 1 cm represents 1 m in the park. Students will locate the point that is 8 cm away in many different locations.

The Park

Anita (*A*), Beth (*B*), and Chen (*C*) play with a Frisbee in the park. To compensate for their different ages, they agree to stand at the positions shown. The arrows show the direction of the Frisbee throws.

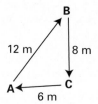

6. a. Who throws the Frisbee to whom?

b. Which player throws the farthest?

c. Make a scale drawing showing the relative positions of *A*, *B*, and *C*. Don't forget to include the scale on your drawing.

You probably noticed it is difficult to draw the distances between the people accurately.

The line on **Student Activity Sheet 2** is a scale drawing of Beth and Anita's positions in the park.

7. a. What is the scale on **Student Activity Sheet 2** for the 12 m distance between Beth and Anita?

b. On **Student Activity Sheet 2**, find a position for Chen that is exactly 8 meters (m) from Beth. Explain how you determined Chen's position.

Reaching All Learners

Intervention

You may need to remind students how a scale is indicated using a scale line or a double number line. Students learned about these number tools in the unit *Models You Can Count On*.

Act It Out

Use three ropes or strong cords of lengths 6 m, 8 m, and 12 m. Then have the students form the triangle, using the ropes as the sides. They can get a mental picture of what the triangle should look like. You might need to use lengths of 6 ft, 8 ft, and 12 ft so the triangle will fit in your classroom.

Solutions and Samples

6. a. Anita to Beth; Beth to Chen; Chen to Anita

b. Player A (Anita).

c. Drawings will vary. Students may have used different scales. See answer for problem 7a for different ways of indicating the scale. Sample drawing:

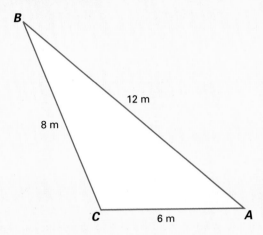

7. a. Students may have used different ways to describe the scale.

Using a scale line:

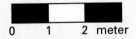

Or a double number line:

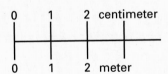

Or using words:

Each centimeter on the drawing represents one meter in the park.

b. Most students will explain that they used a ruler to find a point at a distance of 8 cm from point B.

Hints and Comments

Materials
Student Activity Sheet 2 (one per student); centimeter ruler (one per student)

Overview
Students try to make a correct scale drawing of the relative positions of three Frisbee throwers with given distances between them.

About the Mathematics
Students are slowly led to the idea of using a pair of compasses to construct a triangle given the lengths of the three sides.

Planning
Students may work on problems 6 and 7 in small groups to discuss their answers.

Comments About the Solutions

6. c. The purpose of this problem is for students to learn how difficult it is to construct a triangle with exact measurements. Allow students to work long enough to understand the need for a better method than trial-and-error, but not so long that they become frustrated.

7. a. Students should use a centimeter ruler to answer this question.

b. Some students may label a point in the tree area, which is fine.

Notes

7e You may need to ask if the possible locations for Chen form a shape. They should notice that the points form part of a circle with a radius of 8 cm.

8a Safety compasses work fine, but a string attached to a pencil will also work if you do not have compasses.

9b Encourage students to make a sketch to help them analyze this problem. Remind them that Chen throws 6 m and Anita throws 12 m.

They could model it with toothpicks or string cut the appropriate lengths.

   c. Using the position you determined for Chen, find the distance from Chen to Anita.

   d. Determine and label another position for Chen that is 8 m from Beth. Using this new position for Chen, find the distance from Chen to Anita.

   e. Try several more locations for Chen that are 8 m from Beth. Describe and explain any pattern that emerges from finding more locations for Chen.

A compass is a useful tool for the previous activity. A compass makes it easier to draw all the possible locations that are 8 m away from Beth.

8. a. Use a compass and **Student Activity Sheet 2** to find all possible positions that are 8 m from Beth.

   b. Now use a compass to draw all possible positions that are 6 m from Anita on **Student Activity Sheet 2**.

   c. Find a point that is 8 m from Beth and 6 m from Anita.

   d. If Anita, Beth, and Chen play in an area that is not blocked by trees on one side, how many locations are possible for Chen?

Beth has to go home. Anita and Chen look for a new player. They realize a new player will likely require a new throwing arrangement. Chen was feeling good about his game and asked Anita to keep the distance between them the same.

9. a. Faji usually throws the Frisbee a distance of 20 m. Should Anita and Chen invite Faji to play with them? Explain.

   b. What is the range of the distances that the third player could throw in order to join Anita and Chen?

Assessment Pyramid

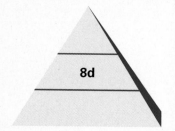

8d

Use a compass to solve problems.

Reaching All Learners

Act It Out

Students might benefit from a demonstration with rope lengths.
One person can be Beth and stay fixed in one position, holding one end of an 8-m (or -ft) rope. Another person holding the other end of the rope can walk and show the circular path. Be sure the rope remains tight so the two people remain the same distance apart.

For problem 9 the two ropes of lengths 6 and 12 could help students figure out the range of distances that the third player could throw. Have three students hold the two ropes taut and figure out the maximum and minimum distance for the third side.

Solutions and Samples

7. c.–d. Answers will vary. The distance from Chen to Anita could range from 4 m (distance AC_1) to 20 m (distance AC_2).

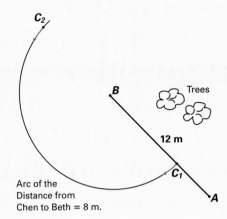

Arc of the Distance from Chen to Beth = 8 m.

e. The points form a circle with a radius of 8 m. Some students may note that it is not a complete circle because it runs through the tree area, which is fine.

8. a.–c.

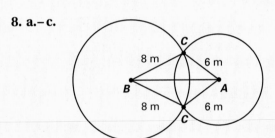

d. There are two possible locations (C) for Chen, as shown in the picture.

9. a. Answers may vary. Sample student responses:

Yes, as long as the person is willing to throw less than the full 20 m. Actually, the person would have to throw less than 18 m to play.

No, that is too far for any triangle with A and C. If the distance between C and A is 6 m and the distance between A and the new player is 12 m, then the distance between the new player and C must be less than 6+12, or 18 m. If the new player is 20 m from Chen, Anita will not be able to throw far enough to reach him or her.

b. Anywhere between 6 and 18 m.

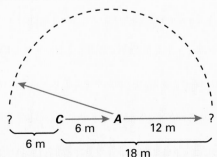

Hints and Comments

Materials

Student Activity Sheet 2 (one per student); compass (one per student); centimeter ruler (one per student) rope (optional)

Overview

Students start to use a pair of compasses to construct triangles in order to determine possible relative locations for three Frisbee throwers who can throw given distances.

Planning

When students finish problem 7, you may want to have a class discussion about the problem. Problem 7e leads nicely to the introduction of the use of a pair of compasses. You may want to have students practice drawing circles with a compass before they start problem 8.

Comments About the Solutions

7. c.–d. Students should get a picture of all the possible positions for Chen.

e. This question is leading up to the compass construction of a triangle when the lengths of all three sides are known. Some students may note that a circle is the set of points that are a certain distance (radius) from a point.

9. a. Students may solve this problem by sketching the possible locations for each player or by reasoning based on the rule for the lengths of sides of triangles. If students have difficulty, you might encourage them to sketch the situation using a compass.

b. Note that C cannot be exactly 6 m or 18 m away from A, because that would make a flat triangle. Points A, B, and C would be standing exactly in line.

Notes

Suppose the sides of a triangle have the lengths $AB = 7$ centimeters (cm), $AC = 5$ cm, and $BC = 6$ cm.

10. a. Draw side AB on a blank piece of paper.

b. From B, use a compass to find all possible locations of C.

c. From A, use a compass to find all possible locations of C.

d. Reflect After the spaghetti activity, you stated a requirement for making triangles. Describe how a compass could be used to illustrate this requirement.

The table lists sets of lengths that may or may not form triangles.

	Length (in cm)		
	Side *AB*	Side *BC*	Side *AC*
Set 1	16	14	8
Set 2	24	10	12
Set 3	20	15	16
Set 4	13	7	21

11 For the ones that are not possible, have students explain why they are impossible.

11. Without drawing them, tell which sets form triangles. Construct one of these triangles on paper.

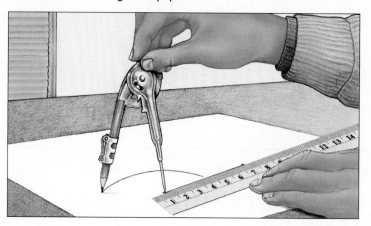

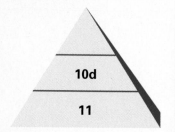
Reaching All Learners

Intervention

Some students may find it easier to first identify the two shortest side lengths and add them so they do not miss that combination.

Solutions and Samples

10. a.-c.

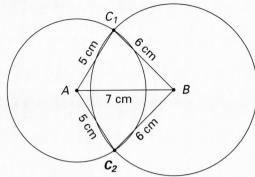

d. Explanations will vary. Sample explanation:

Two circles drawn at the endpoints need to be big enough so that they touch. They must touch in two places; if they touch in only one place, the sides are not long enough to form a triangle.

11. Sets 1 and 3 form triangles. Sets 2 and 4 do not form triangles because each has a side that is larger than the sum of the other two sides. Sample drawings:

Set 1:

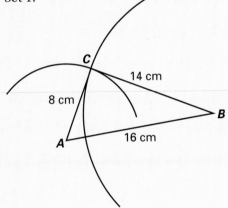

Set 3:

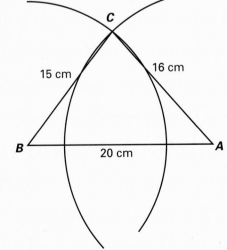

Hints and Comments

Materials

centimeter ruler (one per student); compass (one per student)

Overview

Students construct a triangle with given side lengths. They determine, without drawing, which sets of given side lengths will form triangles.

Comments About the Solutions

10. a.–c.

Students should focus on the triangle, not the circles. After some practice, they should need to make only short arcs instead of entire circles.

d. If students have difficulty, you might remind them of the requirement they discovered in the spaghetti activity. Using a compass to construct triangles enables students to reflect on their earlier discovery.

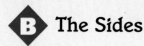
Notes

This is a good time to have students review their vocabulary cards or posters if they made them.

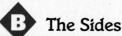
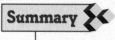

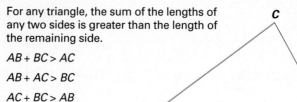

For any triangle, the sum of the lengths of any two sides is greater than the length of the remaining side.

$AB + BC > AC$

$AB + AC > BC$

$AC + BC > AB$

If you have three side lengths *and* the lengths satisfy the conditions above, you can use a compass and straightedge to construct the triangle.

There are three ways to classify a triangle according to the side lengths.

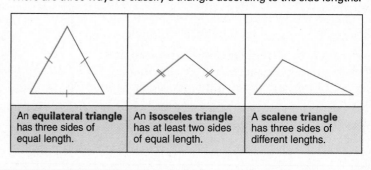

An **equilateral triangle** has three sides of equal length.	An **isosceles triangle** has at least two sides of equal length.	A **scalene triangle** has three sides of different lengths.

Reaching All Learners

English Language Learners

Students may benefit from writing the terms *equilateral, isosceles,* and *scalene* and having a partner draw an example of each.

Hints and Comments

Overview

Students read the Summary, which reviews the main concepts covered in this section.

Notes

1 If students have difficulty getting started, advise them to choose a side length and begin by drawing that line segment.

2 You could ask students to do just one or both possibilities.

3 You may want to encourage students to include a sketch in their explanations.

Check Your Work

1. Construct an isosceles triangle and an equilateral triangle using only a compass and a straightedge, not a ruler.

2. Charlene has two pieces of uncooked spaghetti. One has a length of 5 cm; the other has a length of 3 cm. She cuts a third piece so she can make an isosceles triangle. Make an accurate drawing of Charlene's triangle.

3. Aaron wants to make a triangle using three straws. The longest straw is 10 cm. The other two straws are 4 cm each. Explain why Aaron cannot form a triangle with his three straws. Explain how he can change the length of one straw to make a triangle.

 For Further Reflection

Is it possible that one triangle would fit the definition for two types of triangles? If so, write a statement that shows this double identity.

Assessment Pyramid

Assesses Section B Goals

Reaching All Learners

Intervention

If any students are struggling with number 3, allow them to model it with straws. Advise them to reread the definitions on page 14 if they cannot get started on the For Further Reflection question. If necessary, ask what is meant by "at least" in the definition of an isosceles triangle.

Solutions and Samples

Answers to Check Your Work

1. Triangles will vary in size.

   To construct an isosceles triangle, you draw one side length. Then you use a compass to mark the same distance away from each end of this side. Finally, connect the ends to where the arcs meet.

   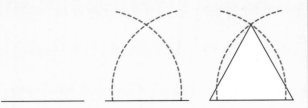

   To construct an equilateral triangle, you begin with one side length. Then you open the compass to this side length. To make sure it fits exactly, use your compass to mark each end of the side. Finally, from each end, mark off this same distance. Connect the ends to where the arcs meet.

   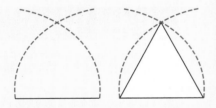

2. Two triangles are possible:

   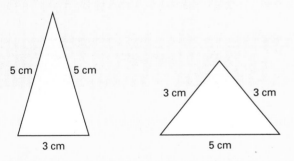

3. Aaron cannot form a triangle with the three straws because the sum of the lengths of the two shortest straws is less than the length of the third straw, so they cannot meet to form a triangle.

   Aaron will have to cut the 10-cm straw so that it is less than 8 cm long. One possibilty is to cut off 3 cm and make a triangle with the two 4-cm straws and the 7-cm straw.

For Further Reflection

Yes. Sample statement:

An equilateral triangle is also an isosceles triangle.

Hints and Comments

Materials

centimeter ruler (one per student); compass (one per student)
Straws (optional)

Check Your Work Problems

These problems are designed for student self-assessment. A student who can answer the questions correctly has understood enough of the concepts taught in the section to be able to start the next section. Students who have difficulties in answering the questions without help may need extra practice. This section is also useful for parents who want to help their children with their work.

Answers are provided in the Student Book. Have students discuss their answers with classmates.

After students complete Section B, you may assign appropriate activities from the Additional Practice section, located on page 54 of the *Triangles and Beyond* Student Book, for homework.

Comments About the Solutions

1. If students have difficulty, you might advise them to begin by drawing a line segment.

2. If students come up with just one isosceles triangle, you may encourage them to find a second possible isosceles triangle.

3. You may want to have students make drawings to illustrate their answers.

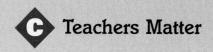
Section Focus

Students explore the angles of a triangle. They cut out three angles that are 180° together to create a triangle, and they discover that three angle pieces whose measures total more than 180° will not make a triangle. They also see that cutting of the three angles of a triangle will produce angle pieces that form a semicircle. Students investigate the properties of isosceles and equilateral triangles with respect to the angle measurements. At the end of the section they apply what they have learned to calculate angles of triangles. The instructional focus of Section C is to:

- **investigate and apply the geometric property that the sum of the angles in a triangle is 180°;**

- **construct a triangle from two angles and one side; and**

- **investigate and apply the geometric property that the longest (shortest) side of a triangle is opposite the largest (smallest) angle.**

Pacing and Planning

Day 6: Parallel Lines and Triangles		Student pages 16 and 17
ACTIVITIES	Problems 1–3	Cut a semicircle into three wedges and arrange the angles to form a triangle.
CLASSWORK	Problems 4	Discuss the geometric property that the sum of the angles in a triangle is 180°.
HOMEWORK	Problems 5 and 6	Test a geometric property by trying to find a counterexample.

Day 7: Starting with a Semicircle		Student pages 18–20
INTRODUCTION	Problem 7	Identify geometric properties.
CLASSWORK	Problems 8–12	Construct a triangle from one side and two angles; and investigate the properties of an isosceles triangle.
HOMEWORK	Problem 13	Describe properties of an isosceles triangle.

Day 8: Triangles and Angles		Student pages 20–23
INTRODUCTION	Review homework.	Review homework from Day 7.
CLASSWORK	Problem 14	Find angle values for a triangle, given information about other angles and sides.
HOMEWORK	Check Your Work; For Further Reflection	Student self-assessment: Construct a triangle from three given sides.

Day 9: Summary		Student pages 21–23
REVIEW	Sections A–C review	Review Summary pages and geometric properties from Sections A through C.
ASSESSMENT	Quiz #1	Assesses Section A through C goals.

Additional Resources: Additional Practice Section C, page 56

Materials

Student Resources
Quantities listed are per student.

- Student Activity Sheets 3–5

Teachers Resources
No resources required.

Student Materials
Quantities listed are per pair of students, unless otherwise noted.

- Centimeter ruler
- Drawing paper (one per student)
- Protractor or compass card
- Scissors

* See Hints and Comments for optional materials.

Learning Lines

Properties, Similar and Congruent Triangles

When students create a triangle from three angle pieces whose measures total 180°, they will notice that they can make smaller and larger triangles using the same three pieces. This activity is also related to the similarity postulate AAA (Angle-Angle-Angle): For any two triangles, if the corresponding angles are congruent, then the triangles are similar. Note that the activity in Section B with the pieces of uncooked spaghetti is related to the SSS (Side-Side-Side) postulate: Two triangles are congruent if three sides of one triangle are congruent to three sides of the other triangle. The development of the concept of congruency starts in Section E. Similarity and congruency are investigated more formally in the unit *It's All the Same.*

Proofs

The sum of the three angles of a triangle is 180°. At an informal level, students explored this property in the unit Looking at an Angle. In this unit, there are different ways to show that cutting the three angles of a triangle forms a semicircle. This is not a formal proof, but for students it is a useful way to demonstrate the plausibility of this property. A more formal proof is based on one of the properties of parallel lines and equal angles.

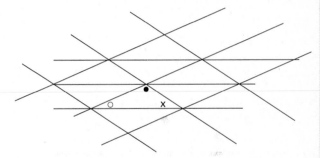

Notation

The symbol $\triangle$ for the word *triangle* is introduced.

At the End of This Section: Learning Outcomes

Students know and can use the properties of the sides and angles of isosceles and equilateral triangles. Students know and can use the rule that the sum of the angle measurements in a triangle is 180°.

Notes

An interesting way to begin this section is with a discussion of 360° and 180° turns. Students are usually familiar with this vocabulary from skateboarding, ice-skating, or roller-skating. They could demonstrate with their bodies, then draw a 180° angle on their paper.

Angles and Triangles

Parallel Lines and Angles

In Section A, you studied families of parallel lines. Here are three families of parallel lines.

1. **a.** On **Student Activity Sheet 3**, use the symbols ● and O and **X** to mark all angles that have the same measure.

   b. Use your drawing to explain why ● + O + **X** = 180°.

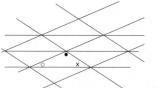

Activity

Starting with a Semicircle

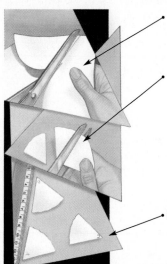

i. Cut a semicircle from a piece of paper. You don't have to be very precise, but it helps to use the edge of the paper for the straight side of the semicircle.

ii. Select a point along the straight side of the semicircle. Draw two lines through this point. Before cutting, label each section near the point using the letters *A*, *B*, and *C*. Cut the semicircle into three pieces.

iii. Create triangle *ABC* by rearranging the three pieces. It helps to have the rounded edges inward. Sketch the triangle.

Assessment Pyramid

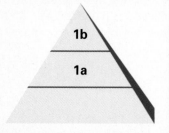

Develop general statements for geometric relationships.

Describe angle relationships.

Reaching All Learners

Intervention

Knowing exactly what is meant by the term *angle* is difficult for some students. They might need several different models to understand this term. Some possibilities are using two strips of poster board hooked together with a brad so the strips can be moved like the rays of an angle. The hands of a clock could also be used. Have students model angles of various sizes.

Solutions and Samples

1. a.

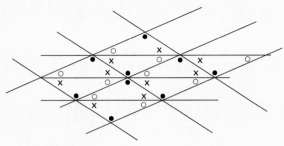

b. Different explanations are possible.

For example, you can use the idea that six angles together make 360°. (See the colored area in the picture below.)

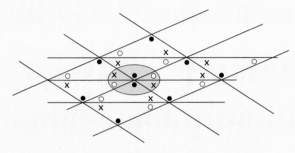

Thus ● + ● + ○ + ○ + X + X = 360°,

So ● + ○ + X = 180°.

Another possibility is that you take three angles that form a semicircle.

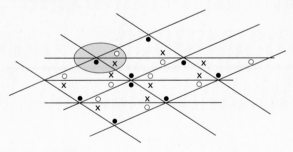

So ● + X + ○ = 180°.

Hints and Comments

Materials

Student Activity Sheet 3 (one per student); drawing paper (one sheet per student); centimeter ruler (one per student); scissors (one pair per student)

Overview

Students review families of parallel lines and use the properties of parallel lines to find equal angles. Then they cut a semicircle into three pieces and form triangles using the pieces.

About the Mathematics

In problem 1 and in the activity that is continued on the next page, students use their knowledge that a semicircle measures 180°.

Students will describe a geometric property about angles and triangles on the next page.

Comments About the Solutions

1. Students should use the property of parallel lines rather than measuring the angles. (Parallel lines form equal angles with a line that intersects them.)

   The focus of this problem is to review the angle measurement of a semicircle.

   This problem actually is a kind of proof of the geometric property that the sum of the angles of a triangle is 180°. However, do not discuss this here, but reflect on problem 1 at the end of the section or when a class discussion of one of the other problems asks for a more formal proof.

Activity

When students create a triangle from the three angle pieces, they may notice that they can make smaller and larger triangles using the same pieces. You may discuss their results so they will be aware of this.

Angles and Triangles

Notes

iv. Now move the pieces a little farther apart and closer together to make larger and smaller triangles. Sketch each of these triangles.

v. Repeat the steps using a different semicircle. Describe your results. Keep these pieces handy for future work.

2. Can you cut a semicircle into three pieces that will not form a triangle? Explain. Assume that the pieces were cut using the directions from this activity.

3. From the activity, you might have discovered some geometric properties about angles and triangles. Summarize your discoveries in your notebook.

This drawing represents a geometric property about three angles cut from a semicircle. The sum of the three angles is 180°.

4 You may want the students to measure each angle, record the measurement, and make sure the total is 180°. This is helpful for doing problems 5 and 6.

5 Students could tape the angles on their papers to show what happens when the total is more than 180°.

4. Use this information to rewrite the geometric property you described in problem 3.

Find the semicircle pieces from the previous activity.

5. Select three angle pieces whose measures total more than 180°. Try to make a triangle with them. Is this possible? How can you be sure?

6. Select three angles whose measures total less than 180°. Try to make a triangle with them. Is this possible? How can you be sure?

Assessment Pyramid

Develop general statements for geometric relationships.

Reaching All Learners

Extension

For the semicircle activity, student groups could create posters of results. Have students examine various possibilities: a semicircle with one obtuse angle, a semicircle with a 90° angle, and a semicircle with three acute angles. Record the angle measurements inside each angle and add the total. Add the property they discover to their poster.

Solutions and Samples

2. No, any combination of angles cut this way from a semicircle will form a triangle.

3. Answers will vary. Sample response:

With every set of three angles that are cut from a semicircle, a triangle can be made.

4. Answers will vary. Sample response:

If you have three angles with measurements that add up to 180°, you can make a triangle from them.

5. No, a triangle cannot be formed because it can only be done when the angle pieces measure exactly 180°.

6. No, a triangle cannot be formed because it can only be done when the angle pieces measure exactly 180°.

Hints and Comments

Materials

drawing paper (one sheet per student);
centimeter ruler (one per student);
scissors (one pair per student)

Overview

Students cut semicircles into three pieces and make triangles with the pieces. They generalize about their findings and formulate a rule that relates to any semicircle. They also try to find counterexamples.

About the Mathematics

Any semicircle (or "straight" angle) can be cut into three pieces that will form a triangle.

Planning

Students may work on problem 2 in small groups. Problems 3–6 may be done individually.

C Angles and Triangles

Notes

Here is a drawing much like the previous drawing.

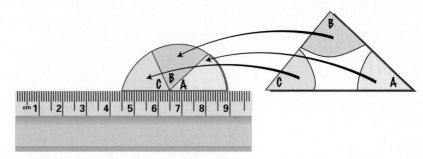

7 This problem is critical. Students are being asked to formulate the main theorem of this section.

7a Ask students to observe what is different between the drawing on page 17 and the one on page 18.

7b You may want to make a poster (or have a student make a poster) of this important property.

7. a. What geometric property of triangles is pictured?

b. Reflect Describe how these two properties and the two pictures are related.

Here is triangle *PQR*.

P, *Q*, and *R* are the names of the vertices of the triangle.

∠*P* is a shorter notation for the angle at **vertex** *P*.

You can replace the word *triangle* with a △ symbol. Instead of writing *triangle PQR*, you can write △ *PQR*.

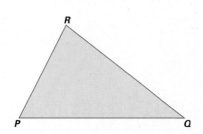

Assessment Pyramid

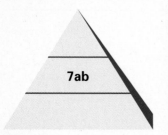

Describe geometric figures using words and diagrams.

Reaching All Learners

Intervention

Some students may need prompting for problem 7a. Ask questions such as: *What are* A, B, *and* C? *How does the ruler show something special about the measures of angles* A, B, *and* C? Remind them that the ruler is not being used for measurement. It is used to show a straight line.

Parent Involvement

Students may show their family the "proof" that is shown in problem 7 by tearing off the angles of a triangle and lining up the angles along a straightedge. Allow students to practice in class.

Solutions and Samples

7. a. The sum of the three angles of a triangle is 180°.

b. The second picture is the reverse of the first one.

The two properties are reverse statements:

- If you have three angles with measurements that add up to 180°, you can make a triangle from them.

- If you have a triangle, then the angles are together a straight angle (180°).

Hints and Comments

Materials

drawing paper (optional, one sheet per student); centimeter ruler (optional, one per student); scissors (optional, one pair per student)

Overview

Students describe a drawing that represents the geometric property of triangles: when the three angles from a triangle are put together, they form a semicircle.

Students learn the symbols for *angle* ($\angle P$) and *triangle* ($\triangle PQR$).

About the Mathematics

The drawing on this page (the three angles from a triangle are put together, and they form a semicircle) shows the reverse of the drawing on the previous page (a semicircle is cut into three pieces, and they form a triangle).

Planning

Problem 7 can be used as informal assessment. Discuss the notations for angle and triangle.

Comments About the Solutions

7. Again, this drawing does not provide a formal proof, but it does help to make the idea more concrete for students.

◆C◆ Angles and Triangles

Notes

You may want to give students a copy of this page so they can cut it apart to form triangle *ABC*.

8a Have them first determine the measurements of angles *A*, *B*, and *C* using the equal sections of the grid. Then let them use a protractor or circle compass to compare the results. They should also check to see if the sum of the measures is 180°.

8b Before they draw side *AC*, remind students they need room for *A*, so they need to allow enough space for this. Be sure they label the end points with the letters *A* and *C*.

8c Students should use a protractor to construct angle *A* or tape angle *A* from their cut-out onto point angle *A*.

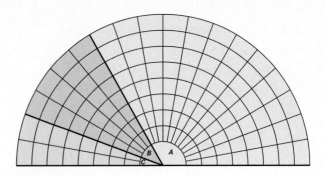

Here are three angles: ∠*A*, ∠*B*, and ∠*C*.

They are drawn in a semicircle that has been subdivided into equal parts. They can be cut apart and put together to form △*ABC*.

8. a. What are the measures of ∠*A*, ∠*B*, and ∠*C*?

  b. Start with a line segment that is 10 cm long and label its ends *A* and *C*.

  c. ∠*A* occurs at point *A*. Draw ∠*A* on your piece of paper.

  d. Finish drawing △*ABC*.

  e. Is it necessary to use the measures of all three angles to complete your triangle? Explain why or why not.

  f. There are many different triangles with the same three angle measures you drew in part **d**. Draw another △ *ABC*, this time with a different length for side *AC*. Compare your triangle to a classmate's drawing. Describe any similarities and differences among the three triangles.

Triangles and Angles

Here is an isosceles triangle. The slashes on the sides show which two sides are of equal length.

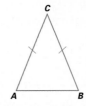

9. a. In △*ABC*, name the shortest side. Name the angle opposite this shortest side.

  b. Name the angles opposite sides *AC* and *BC*.

  c. Describe any relationship between the two angles.

  d. Which angle is smaller: ∠*A* or ∠*C*? How can you be sure without measuring it directly?

Assessment Pyramid

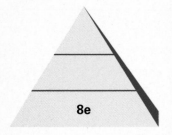

8e

Use properties of triangles.

Reaching All Learners

Extension

For homework, assign students other lengths for side *AC*, such as 6 cm or 20 cm, and repeat the directions a through d. Then ask what they observe about all these triangles with the same three angle measures. You could mention that the mathematical term for this is *similar triangles*. They will study this more in depth in the unit *It's All the Same*.

Solutions and Samples

8. a. $\angle A = 120°$

   $\angle B = 40°$

   $\angle C = 20°$

b.

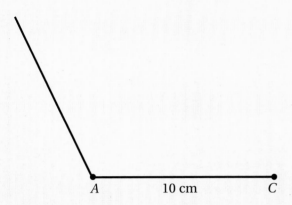

A 10 cm C

c.

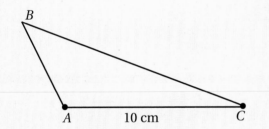

A 10 cm C

d.

B

A 10 cm C

e. No. The minimum information needed in this case is the length of side AC and the measurements of $\angle A$ and either $\angle B$ or $\angle C$.

f. The triangles have the same shape and differ only in size. Or: they are enlargements or reductions of each other.

9. a. The shortest side is side AB. The angle opposite this side is $\angle C$.

b. Opposite AC is $\angle B$; opposite BC is $\angle A$.

c. $\angle B$ is equal to $\angle A$.

d. Answers will vary. Sample responses:

You can trace $\angle A$, and $\angle C$ is smaller than $\angle A$ because the side opposite $\angle C$ is smaller than the side opposite $\angle A$.

Hints and Comments

Materials

centimeter ruler (one per student); protractor or compass card, (one per student)

Overview

Students find the measurements for three angles. They construct a triangle using these measurements and the length of one side.

About the Mathematics

When students create a triangle from three angle pieces whose measures total 180°, they will notice that they can make smaller and larger triangles using the same three pieces. Students describe similar triangles using their own words. The word *similar* is not made explicit; however, you could mention it depending on your students' ability to handle more formal language.

This activity is also related to the similarity postulate AAA (Angle-Angle-Angle): For any two triangles, if the corresponding angles are congruent, then the triangles are similar.

Planning

Students may work on problem 12 in small groups. Discuss students' answers.

The Extension described on the next page can be assigned as homework.

Comments About the Solutions

8. a. Students may use protractors, or they may use the grid on page 19 to measure the angles. The grid is divided into 18 equal angles so that each section is 10°. Students should check to see whether the three angles add up to 180°.

b. Students need to use a centimeter ruler to draw side AC.

c. Encourage students to use protractors or compass cards to draw $\angle A$, instead of tracing it.

Angles and Triangles

Notes

10a Students may use one letter to name the angle or three letters. Be sure they know that if they use three letters, the letter for the vertex must be in the middle.

11 Some students may already know the term *line of symmetry* and mention it at this time.

12 Encourage students to show how they would calculate their answer.

13 Have students add this information to their vocabulary poster or vocabulary cards if they made them.

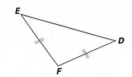

10. a. In △*DEF*, name the longest side and name the angle opposite the longest side.

b. What do you know about the sides that are opposite the other two angles? Describe any relationship between the angles.

Activity

Investigate the properties of isosceles triangles with a right angle.

11. a. Fold the isosceles triangle in half. What geometric property about isosceles triangles did you illustrate?

b. Investigate the properties of an isosceles triangle with a right angle. How is this isosceles triangle different from any isosceles triangle? How is it the same?

12. What can you conclude about the angles of an equilateral triangle? Be prepared to use your equilateral triangle to demonstrate your conclusions.

13. Copy and complete the sentences describing the angles of isosceles and equilateral triangles.

In an isosceles triangle,…

In an equilateral triangle,…

Assessment Pyramid

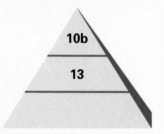

Develop general statements for geometric relationships.

Describe geometric figures using words.

Reaching All Learners

English Language Learners

Explain what is meant by the term *relationship*. Ask, *Is one angle larger than the other or are they equal in size?*

Intervention

For problem 12, you may want to provide students with a copy of an equilateral triangle and give them an opportunity to fold it and check for congruent angles and sides and explore the lines of symmetry.

Solutions and Samples

10. a. The longest side is *DE*, and the angle opposite this side is ∠*F*.

b. The sides that are opposite the other two angles are equal.

∠*D* is equal to ∠*E*.

∠*D* and ∠*E* are both smaller than ∠*F*.

11. a. By folding the triangle over the centerline, you can see that the measure of ∠*A* equals the measure of ∠*B*.

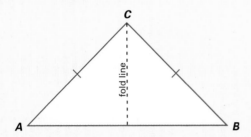

b. Some students might notice an isosceles right triangle looks like half of a square. All isosceles triangles have two equal angles as well as two equal sides.

12. The three angles have equal measures. Every triangle has angles with measures that total 180°. Therefore, every angle of an equilateral triangle must measure 180° ÷ 3 = 60°.

13. In an isosceles triangle, the angles opposite the two equal sides have the same measure.

In an equilateral triangle, all the angles have the same measure. Each angle is 60°.

Hints and Comments

Materials

centimeter ruler (one per student);
scissors (one pair per student);
tracing paper (optional, one sheet per student);
protractor or compass card (one per student)

Overview

Students explore the properties of the angles of isosceles and equilateral triangles

About the Mathematics

Students informally use the Opposite Parts theorem, which students will meet again in Section D. "The longest side of a triangle is opposite the largest angle." This theorem (sometimes named the Hinge theorem) can be used to establish that a triangle with equal base angles (isosceles) has two equal sides (and vice versa), and that a triangle with all angles equal (equilateral) has three equal sides (and vice versa).

Planning

You may want to start this page with the Extension below or with a discussion of it if it was homework. Students may work on problems 10–13 individually or in small groups. Problem 13 may be used as informal assessment.

Extension

This problem will also give students an extra opportunity to measure angles using a protractor or a compass card.

- Draw two large triangles. Measure the angles and the sides of the triangles and write the results in your drawing.

- With one color, mark the smallest angles and the shortest sides. With a different color, mark the largest angles and the longest sides.

- What geometric property of triangles do you notice?

Notes

14 You may want to ask students what the slashes indicate and what that means for the angles.

You may want to see how students solve the first problem before you assign the others as homework. Make sure that students can explain how they found their answers.

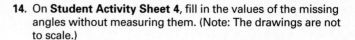

14. On **Student Activity Sheet 4**, fill in the values of the missing angles without measuring them. (Note: The drawings are not to scale.)

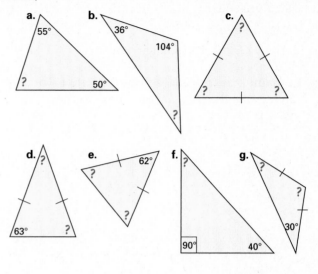

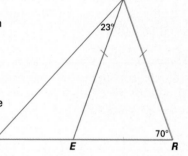

15. **a.** How many triangles can you find in this figure? Classify the triangles.

   b. Make a sketch of each triangle.

   c. Find the size of the three angles of each triangle.

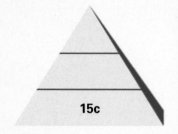

Reaching All Learners

Intervention

Students might color the two equal angles in the isosceles triangles in problem 14 to help them notice the difference between them. When they have their solution, they can then check to see if their equal numbers are in the correct places.

Solutions and Samples

14. a.–g.

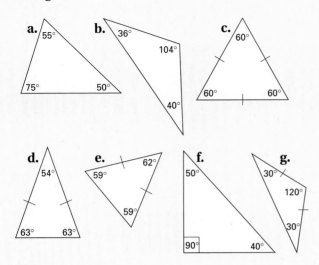

15. a. There are three triangles:

△*VRO*, △*ERO*, and △*VEO*.

△*VRO* is scalene;

△*ERO* is isosceles;

△*VEO* is scalene.

b. and **c.**

Sample calculations:

in △*ERO*: ∠*E* = ∠*R* = 70°

∠*O* = 180° − (70° + 70°) = 40°

in △*VRO*: ∠*R* = 70°

∠*O* = 23° + 40° = 63°

∠*V* = 180° − (70° + 63°) = 47°

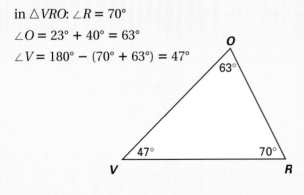

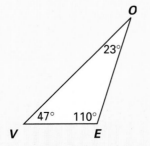

Hints and Comments

Materials

Student Activity Sheet 4 (one per student)
colored pencils

Overview

Students solve problems using the properties of
triangles they discovered in this section.

Planning

Problems 14 and 15 may be done individually.
They may also be assigned as homework.

Comments About the Solutions

14. Since students cannot measure the angles, they
will have to find the values by reasoning.
For example, the missing angle in problem 14a
can be found by subtracting the sum of the two
given angles from 180°:

180° − (55° + 50°) = 180° − 105° = 75°.

In problem 14c, students may use the information
that the three sides are equal to conclude that
the three angles are equal. Since the three angles
in every triangle add up to 180°, each angle
measures 60°.

Students may conclude that since the triangle
in problem 14g is isosceles, one of the missing
angles measures 30°, and the other must measure

180° − (30° + 30°) = 120°.

15. This is a more complex situation. In order to give
students an idea how to solve this type of problem,
they are asked to draw all the triangles they see in
the picture.

Calculations can be made differently. However,
students have to start with △*ERO*. Then they can
either continue with △*ERO* or with △*VRO*.

Notes

This would be a good
opportunity to have
students review the
properties learned so far
in this unit.

Have students reread the
Summary for Sections A,
B, and C as review before
taking Quiz 1.

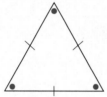

If the measures of three angles
total 180°, then a triangle can be
made with these angles.

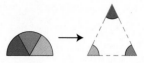

If the measures of three angles
do not total 180°, then a triangle
cannot be made with these angles.

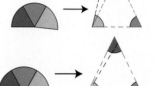

Here is triangle *PQR*. *P*, *Q*, and *R* are
the names of the vertices of the triangle.

$\angle P$ is a shorter notation for the
angle at vertex *P*. Instead of the
word *triangle*, you can use the
symbol $\triangle$; instead of writing
triangle PQR, we can write $\triangle PQR$.

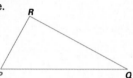

The sum of the measures of the three angles of any triangle is 180°,
so for $\triangle PQR$, you can write $\angle P + \angle Q + \angle R = 180°$.

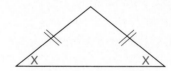

Equilateral triangles have
three equal sides and
three equal angles.

Isosceles triangles have at
least two equal sides and
two equal angles.

Equal angles and equal sides can be indicated by the same symbols.

Reaching All Learners

Act It Out

You might have groups of students present or act out the information in the
Summary using poster-size models of angles and triangles.

Hints and Comments

Overview

Students read the Summary, which reviews the main concepts covered in this section.

Planning

You may have a whole class discussion about "proofs" that show the property for triangles that the sum of the measures of the three angles is 180°.

- They already know how to tear off the three angles: they will make a "stretched" angle of 180°.

- This activity can also be done without tearing off, by folding a triangle:

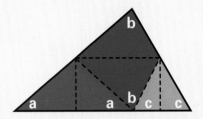

- Ask students to draw a triangle and measure the angles. Do they add up to 180°? If not, explain why the sum will not always be 180°?

- Use the strategy from problem 1 of this section.

Angles and Triangles

Notes

1 The fourth situation is the most complex one. If students have problems solving it, you may help them by questioning. For example, ask, *Why were the first three problems easier to solve?* (Just one triangle, and the measures of two angles were given.) *What did you do in problem 15? Can you use that here?*

2 Encourage students to make a sketch for this so they find both possibilities.

For Further Reflection
After they make their prediction, have students compare several triangles and discuss how they are the same and how they are different. The terms *enlargement* or *reduction* could be mentioned.

Check Your Work

1. On **Student Activity Sheet 5**, fill in the value of the missing angles. The drawings are not to scale, so do not try to measure them to find the answers.

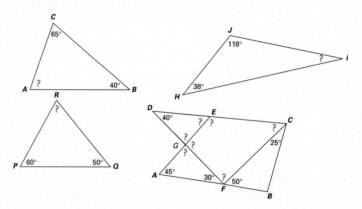

2. △*KLM* is an isosceles triangle, and ∠*K* = 30°. What is the measure of the other angles?

△*XYZ* is a triangle. In △*XYZ*, the measure of ∠*Y* is twice the measure of ∠*X*, and the measure of ∠*Z* is three times ∠*X*.

3. **a.** What is the measure of each angle?

   b. Draw a triangle with these three angle measures.

For Further Reflection

Construct a triangle with angles of 30, 60, and 90 degrees. Without looking at another classmate's drawing, describe how the triangles might be the same and how they might be different.

Assessment Pyramid

1, 2, 3, ◼FFR

Assesses Section C Goals

Reaching All Learners

Intervention

If students are having difficulty getting started on Problem 3, you might suggest they use guess and check or use a ratio table to find the measures. You might also ask what kind of triangle this is and whether there are any angles the same size.

Solutions and Samples

Answers to Check Your Work

1.

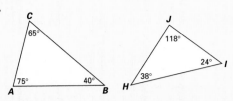

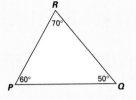

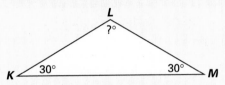

2. The triangle has two equal angles.

One possibility is that the two equal angles are both 30°, and the triangle may look like this.

You know the sum of three angles is 180°, so 30° + 30° + ?° = 180°, and you can find that the third angle is 120°.

Another possibility is that one angle is 30°, and the triangle may look like this.

You know that the other two angles are equal, so you can write:

30° + ?° + ?° = 180°
30° + 150° = 180°

So the other two angles are together 150°, or 75° each.

3. a. ∠X is 30°.

∠Y is 60°.

∠Z is 90°.

A variety of strategies can be used to find the measurement of each angle. Here is one strategy:

∠Y and ∠Z are related to ∠X. ∠Y is twice the size of ∠X, and ∠Z is three times the size of ∠X. So this is like having six ∠X's inside the triangle. 180 ÷ 6 would give the size of ∠X, and that is 30° and twice that is 60° and three times that is 90°.

Hints and Comments

Materials
Student Activity Sheet 5 (one per student); centimeter ruler (one per student); compass card or protractor (one per student)

Check Your Work Problems

These problems are designed for student self-assessment. A student who can answer the questions correctly has understood enough of the concepts taught in the section to be able to start the next section. Students who have difficulties in answering the questions without help may need extra practice.

This section is also useful for parents who want to help their children with their work.

Answers are provided in the Student Book. Have students discuss their answers with classmates.

After students complete Section C, you may assign appropriate activities from the Additional Practice section, located on page 56 of the *Triangles and Beyond* Student Book, for homework.

Comments About the Solutions

1. It is important for students to understand that they have to look for triangles of which the measures of two angles are given so they can calculate the third one.

b.

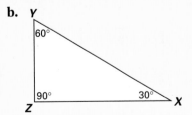

For Further Reflection
Some students may notice that all of the triangles have the same shape, but not the same size. You may want to discuss that this is a key feature of triangles that are similar.

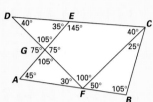

Section Focus

Students investigate the generalization: the longest side of a triangle is opposite the largest angle.

They classify triangles according to the size of the largest angle: acute, right, and obtuse triangles.

Students are introduced to the Pythagorean theorem. By studying the area of squares that fit on the sides of triangles, they will discover that for a right triangle there is a special relationship: If a triangle has a right angle, then the square on the longest side has the same area as the other two squares combined.

Pacing and Planning

Day 10: Squares and Triangles		Student pages 24–26
INTRODUCTION	Problems 1 and 2	Determine the longest side in a triangle using the relative size of angles.
CLASSWORK	Problems 3–5; Make a Poster	Investigate the relationship between the side lengths of a triangle and its angles.

Day 11: Squares and Triangles (continued)		Student pages 27, 28, and 34
INTRODUCTION	Problem 6–8	Classify triangles using their side lengths.
CLASSWORK	Problems 9–11	Investigate the area relationship between squares used to form a triangle.
HOMEWORK	For Further Reflection, Page 34	Reason about using sides and angles to classify triangles.

Day 12: The Pythagorean Theorem		Student pages 29–34
INTRODUCTION	Problems 12 and 13	Investigate essential features of the Pythagorean theorem.
CLASSWORK	Problems 14–16	Use the Pythagorean theorem to find the sides of a right triangle.
HOMEWORK	Check Your Work	Student self-assessment: Apply strategies suggested by the Pythagorean Theorem.

Additional Resources: Additional Practice Section D, page 57

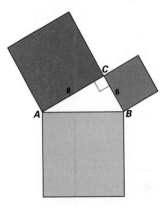
Materials

Student Resources
Quantities listed are per student.

- Student Activity Sheets 6 and 7

Teachers Resources
No resources required.

Student Materials
Quantities listed are per pair of students, unless otherwise noted.

- Calculator (one per student)
- Centimeter graph paper
- Centimeter rulers (one per student)
- Colored markers (two different colors per student)
- One large white paper (poster-size)
- Protractor or compass card
- Scissors
- Straightedge

* See Hints and Comments for optional materials.

Learning Lines

Properties of Triangles

The generalization "The longest side of a triangle is opposite the largest angle." is known as the Opposite Parts theorem or Hinge theorem, but students do not have to know these names.

Measurement, Area, and Length

Students calculate the area of squares drawn on graph paper. They use strategies from the unit *Reallotment* to calculate the area of the squares. Students use the area of a square to find the side length of the square by "unsquaring" or taking the square root of the area. The idea of unsquaring and the square root symbol $\sqrt{}$ was introduced in the unit *Building Formulas*.

The Pythagorean theorem states that in a right triangle, the square of the hypotenuse is equal to the sum of the squares of its legs. In this section, students are informally introduced to the Pythagorean theorem. This means that this theory is described as a relationship of the area of the squares that fit on the sides of a right triangle. This is done to give students visual support and to help them to make their calculations correctly:

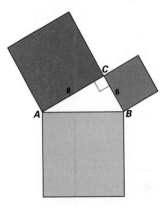

> area of the square on side AC = ...
> area of the square on side BC = ...
> $\qquad\qquad\qquad +$
> ....
> area of the square on side AB = ...
> so AB = ...

Notation

The angle symbol to designate right angles, $\llcorner$, is introduced in this section.

At the End of This Section: Learning Outcomes

Students can recognize and classify acute, right, and obtuse triangles. They are able to use the relationship between the area and the side length of a square. They understand and use the Pythagorean theorem.

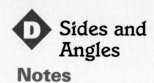

Sides and Angles

Squares and Triangles

1b You might ask if a triangle can contain more than one right angle or more than one obtuse angle and have students explain why not.

In Section B, you created triangles using lengths of uncooked spaghetti. In this section, you will use squares to create triangles.

This figure illustrates how three squares form a triangle.

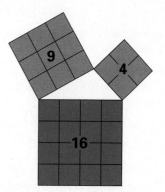

1. **a.** How long is each side of this triangle? How do you know?

   b. Find the largest angle of this triangle.

Triangles can be classified like this: If the largest angle of a triangle is acute, the triangle is called an **acute triangle**.

   c. Define **right triangle** and **obtuse triangle**.

Sylvia notices a geometric property: You can find the largest angle of a triangle opposite the longest side.

   d. Does this property apply to the triangle in the picture above?

2a Discuss ways to check for a right angle without using a protractor, such as using the corner of an index card.

2. **a.** Draw a scalene right triangle. Using the same color, show the triangle's largest angle and longest side. Does Sylvia's property apply to this triangle?

   b. Using a different color, show the triangle's smallest angle and shortest side.

   c. **Reflect** Describe another geometric property related to the right triangle. Write about the geometric properties of an isosceles right triangle.

3 Students may need to use protractors and rulers to verify this.

3. **a.** Draw an acute triangle and investigate whether Sylvia's property also applies to this triangle.

   b. Does the geometric property apply to the acute triangle? Describe where you would find the smallest angle of the triangle.

Assessment Pyramid

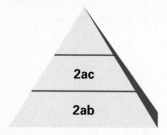

Describe geometric figures using words and diagrams.

Use properties of triangles.

Reaching All Learners

Extension

You could begin this section with students searching for right angles in the classroom. Then have them name some dwellings or buildings that do not contain right angles, such as igloos, tepees, and silos. Students could also find ways right triangles are used in everyday life, such as in trusses or beams.

Vocabulary Building

Add *acute triangle*, *right triangle*, and *obtuse triangle* to your vocabulary poster and have students make vocabulary cards for these terms.

Solutions and Samples

1. a. The sides of the triangle are 2, 3, and 4. The side length of each square can be found by counting the number of "grid squares" that form each side of the triangle.

b. The largest angle is opposite the largest side.

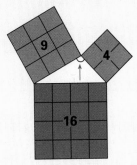

c. A right triangle is a triangle with a right angle (90°).
An obtuse triangle is a triangle with an obtuse angle (more than 90°).

d. Yes, because opposite the largest angle you find a square with an area of 16, and the other squares are smaller, and the largest square has the longest sides.

2. a.

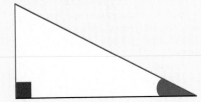

b. The smallest angle is opposite the shortest side.

c. The two angles opposite the shorter sides are both equal. Since they are equal and must add up to 90°, each of the small angles measures 45°. The right angle is opposite the largest side, or opposite of the largest side is the right angle.

3. a.

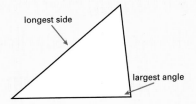

longest side

largest angle

b. Yes, the largest side is opposite the largest angle and the smallest side is opposite the smallest angle.

Hints and Comments

Materials

straightedge (one per student);
compass card or a protractor (one per student);
colored markers (two different colors per student)

Overview

Students start to explore a triangle that is enclosed by three squares. Students define *acute, right,* and *obtuse* triangle. They explore the Opposite Parts theorem: "The longest side of a triangle is opposite the largest angle."

Planning

Students can work in small groups on these problems. You may have a whole class discussion after problem 3. Involve the relationship of the area of the squares and the side lengths in this discussion.

Comments About the Solutions

1. If students do not remember the concepts of obtuse and acute angle from *Figuring All the Angles* you may discuss these concepts first.

3. Students can measure the angles and the sides to find a conclusion.

Notes

Check how well students understand what they have to do before they start cutting out the squares.

Point out that they have to think in advance how all the squares can be cut out in an economical way before they start cutting. The result is ten white squares and ten gray squares. The dimensions of the squares are 1-by-1 tile, 2-by-2 tiles, 3-by-3 tiles, ..., 10-by-10 tiles.

Remind students to save the squares in an envelope or plastic bag to use for activities on pages 26 and 27 and throughout the section.

 Activity

Making Triangles from Squares

For this activity, you need:

- two copies each of **Student Activity Sheet 6** and **Student Activity Sheet 7**;
- scissors; and
- paper.

- Use two copies of **Student Activity Sheet 6** to cut out a sequence of ten white squares representing the first ten perfect square numbers. On each square, write the number of tiles used to make each square. Do the same using two copies of **Student Activity Sheet 7**.

 1 4 9 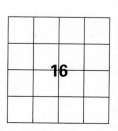 16

- For this activity, you will use one white square and two gray squares to form different triangles. The white square will always form the longest side of the triangle. The two gray squares will always form the shorter sides of the triangle.

 1 4 9 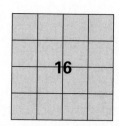 16

Reaching All Learners

Intervention

Have students write the dimensions on each square along with the total number of small squares to reinforce their multiplication facts; for example, 6 by 6 = 36.

Hints and Comments

Materials

Student Activity Sheet 6 and 7 (two of each for each group of students);
scissors (one pair per student)

Overview

Students cut out squares representing the first ten perfect numbers.

About the Mathematics

A perfect square number is a number that is the result of squaring a whole number. For example, $5^2 = 25$, so 25 is a perfect square number.

These numbers also appear when you calculate the area of a square with a whole number as side length.

Planning

You may have students work in pairs on this activity. The activity is continued on the next page.

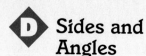
Notes

A good strategy for checking for right angles is to compare the angle with the corner of an index card or a sheet of paper. Those angles that are close to 90° are difficult to determine without a tool.

- Select one white square and two gray squares that can be arranged to make a triangle. Note that each gray square has to be smaller than the white square. Record your results in a table like this. Problem 1 is recorded.

Total Number of Gray Tiles	Total Number of White Tiles	Classification of the Triangle According to Its Largest Angle
4 + 9 = 13	16	obtuse

- Repeat this process for at least five more triangles. Make sure to represent all types of triangles: acute, obtuse, and right.

4. a. Compare your results of the activity to a classmate's results. Describe any patterns in your results.

   b. Describe any special relationship between the white and gray tiles of a right triangle.

Select two gray squares—one with 25 tiles and one with 64 tiles.

5. a. Find the size of a white square that is needed to create an acute triangle.

   b. Find the size of a white square that is needed to create an obtuse triangle.

5 Students may remember from the spaghetti activity that the sum of the lengths of two sides of a triangle has to be greater than the length of the third side.

Reaching All Learners

Intervention

For problem 4a, if students have trouble seeing a pattern, ask them to look at all the acute triangles and see what they notice about the number of gray and white tiles. Then have them look at the right triangles and see what is special about the number of gray and white tiles.

Solutions and Samples

Activity

Sample responses:

Total Number of Gray Tiles	Total Number of White Tiles	Classification of the Triangle According to Its Largest Angle
4 + 9 = 13	16	obtuse
4+16=20	25	obtuse
4+25=29	36	obtuse
9+16=25	25	right
9+25=34	36	obtuse
16+25=41	36	acute
25+36=61	49	acute
36+64=100	100	right

4. a. Answers may vary. Sample responses:

If the total number of gray tiles is different from the total number of white tiles, then the triangle is not a right triangle.

If the total number of gray tiles is less than the total number of white tiles, then the largest angle is obtuse.

If the total number of gray tiles is more than the total number of white tiles, then the largest angle is acute.

b. For right triangles, the total number of gray tiles is equal to the total number of white tiles.

5. a. Possible solutions: a white square of 100 tiles, or one of 144 tiles.

b. A square with 81 tiles (9 by 9).

Hints and Comments

Overview

Students arrange several triangles using one white square and two smaller gray squares. They classify the triangles according to the size of the largest angle. Then they look for relationships between the number of white tiles and the number of gray tiles.

About the Mathematics

In this activity students are informally introduced to the Pythagorean theorem.

The relationships that students discover in this activity are based on the following.

- When the area of the white square is smaller than the area of the two gray squares combined, then the triangle is an acute triangle.
- When the area of the white square is larger than the area of the two gray squares combined, then the triangle is an obtuse triangle.
- When the area of the white square is equal to the area of the two gray squares combined, than the triangle is a right triangle.

Planning

Students can work in pairs when arranging the triangles and then compare their results with another pair of students. You may emphasize that when they select one white and two gray squares, that the white square has to be the largest one.

Discuss students' responses to problem 4 before they continue with problem 5. Then also discuss problem 5.

Comments About the Solutions

5. a. Some students may solve this problem without using the squares. They reason: $25 + 64 = 89$, so the white square must have more than 89 tiles, so a square of 100 tiles is possible. They may find a second solution: a square of 144 tiles.

Note that a white square of 169 tiles cannot be used, because then the three squares cannot form a triangle: $5 + 8 = 13$, and a square of 169 tiles has a side length of 13 tiles.

b. Note that the white square must have more tiles than a gray square.

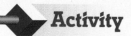
Notes

The posters may be created by groups of students.

6 Recommend that students use the patterns they discovered from the table to classify the triangle. Then students could verify their answer by building the model of it.

7 Remind students to think of the gray and white squares and what they learned from their table. You may need to point out that these are side lengths, not the total number of squares.

Then they could check their solution by using their squares.

Make a Poster

Select squares of various sizes to create three different triangles. Make a poster by pasting the triangles on a large piece of paper. For each triangle, include the following information:

- total number of gray tiles;
- total number of white tiles;
- triangle classification.

6. Classify the triangle formed using one square of 100 tiles, one square of 225 tiles, and one square of 400 tiles.

7. A triangle has the side lengths of 6 cm, 8 cm, and 10 cm. Classify this triangle according to its angles. Explain how you came to this conclusion.

Here is a triangle drawn on grid paper.

8. Use the grid paper to explain why it is an isosceles right triangle.

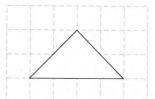

Here is the same isosceles right triangle, but now there is a square on each side.

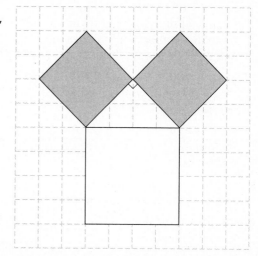

Assessment Pyramid

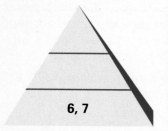

6, 7

Recognize and classify triangles.

Reaching All Learners

Intervention

For problem 8, it may help some students to draw grid lines inside the triangle to see that you have two 45° angles next to each other. Also ask what other name could be given to this right triangle.

Solutions and Samples

6. The largest square has 400 tiles. The other two have $100 + 225 = 325$ tiles together.

400 is more than 325, so the triangle will be obtuse.

7. It is a right triangle.

Sample explanation: The largest side is 10 cm, so the square on that side has an area of 100 cm^2.

The squares on the other sides have together an area of $36 + 64 = 100$ cm^2.

8. Different strategies are possible. Sample strategies:

Using the squares of the grid, you can divide the triangle in smaller triangles that are each half of a square.

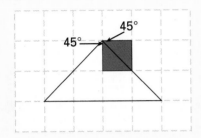

So the angle on top is $45° + 45° = 90°$, so it is a right triangle.

Or four of these triangles make a large square.

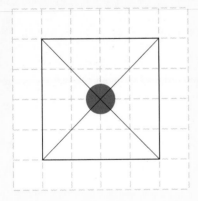

The four angles in the middle are together 360°, so each is $360° \div 4 = 90°$.

Hints and Comments

Materials

large white paper (one sheet per pair of students); centimeter graph paper (one sheet per student); colored pencils (optional)

Overview

Students use the squares from the activity to make a poster that shows the relationships between the tiles of the squares and the kind of triangle they form. Then they classify triangles using this relationship.

About the Mathematics

In problem 8, students start with a right triangle that will be enclosed by squares.

With this problem and the problems on the next page students are informally introduced to the Pythagorean theorem.

Planning

You may have students work in pairs on the poster activity.

Comments About the Solutions

Activity

The results of the poster will show students' understanding of the relationship between the number of tiles of the squares and the kind of triangle they form.

6. and **7.**
These problems assess students' ability to use the relationship between the number of tiles of the squares and the kind of triangle they form and to classify a triangle according to its angles.

8. Students are not supposed to measure the angles using a protractor or a compass card. You may ask students to classify this triangle (a scalene right triangle).
A class discussion gives an opportunity to review the concept of *diagonal*. It should be basic knowledge that folding a square along its diagonal shows that two right angles each are divided in two equal angles of 45°.

Notes

9c If students found the area by counting the squares inside, ask them for another strategy they could have used. (There are two equal areas with a total of 16 squares.)

11c Students may remember how to "unsquare" the area to find the side lengths of the square. If they do not remember, it is not necessary to review this here because it is reviewed on page 30.

Activity

9. **a.** Copy the drawing from page 27.

   b. Find the area of the largest white square.

   c. Find the area of each of the smaller gray squares.

10. Find the area of this white square.

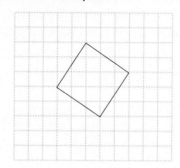

Here is the same white square. Two gray squares were added to form a triangle.

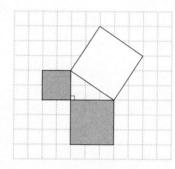

11. **a.** Use the white square and two gray squares to create this triangle on 1-cm grid paper. Label the area of each square.

    b. Describe any relationships you notice between the area of the white square and the area of the gray squares.

    c. Measure the length of the triangle's longest side. Is there another way to find this length? How?

Assessment Pyramid

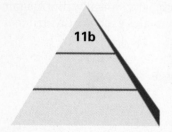

Develop general statements for geometric relationships.

Reaching All Learners

Intervention

For problem 10, suggest that students use the strategies from the unit *Reallotment* to find the area of the square. They could subdivide the square into four congruent triangles with a square in the center, or they could enclose the square inside a larger 5-by-5 square and subtract the areas of the four triangles in the corners. They may need to be reminded that the area of a triangle is half the rectangle enclosing it.

Solutions and Samples

9. a. —

   b. 16 cm²

   c. 8 cm²

Different strategies are possible. Either a student finds the area of a gray square using reallotment, or a student reasons: Since the triangle is a right triangle, the two gray squares have together the same area as the white square, so they are each half of 16 cm², which is 8 cm².

10. The area is 13 cm².

Sample strategies:

Using reallotment:

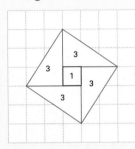

the area =
3 + 3 + 3 + 3 + 1 =
13 cm²

Drawing a square that encloses the given square:

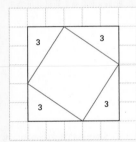

25 − 4 × 3 =
25 − 12 =
13 cm²

11. a. 4 cm² and 9 cm²

   b. The area of the two gray squares together is the same as the area of the white square: 4 + 9 = 13 cm².

   c. The triangle's longest side measures about 3.5 cm.

Another way is unsquaring the area. $\sqrt{13} \approx 3.6$.

Hints and Comments

Materials

centimeter graph paper (one sheet per student)
ruler (one per student)

Overview

Students investigate right triangles and the squares that are drawn on their sides. They find area of squares, and then they focus on the relationship between the area of the squares and the area of the triangle.

About the Mathematics

These problems set the stage to help students to discover and use the Pythagorean theorem.

Students may remember from the unit *Reallotment* how to find the area of a figure drawn on graph paper.

In the unit *Facts and Factors*, students were introduced within the context of area to square and "unsquare." They learned formal notation and used calculators to find square roots.

Planning

Students can work in small groups on these problems. Discuss problem 10 before students continue with problem 11.

Comments About the Solutions

9. b. Students can use reallotment to find the area of the gray squares, or they see that it is half the area of the square that encloses it.

10. Observe students copying the square on graph paper. Some students try to copy it by "sight." It may be helpful to locate the corner points first and then draw the sides. This may students encourage to develop a strategy of counting.

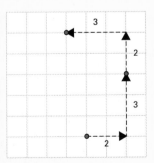

Notes

Students may need to
refer to their table or
poster to see what the
relationship is for right
triangles.

12 In problem 14 on the
next page, students are
asked to find the length
of the longest side using
the square root.

Depending on how much
progress your students
have made, you could
decide to discuss the
square root here.

The Pythagorean Theorem

About 2,500 years ago in Greece,
there lived a famous mathematician,
scientist, and philosopher named
Pythagoras.

Pythagoras described a way of
constructing right angles and the
relationship among the areas of
the three squares. This relationship
is described by the **Pythagorean
theorem**.

This figure shows a right triangle and
three squares.

12. Find the area of the white square.
Show your work.

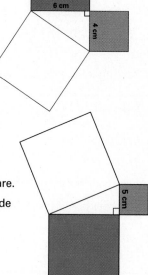

13. a. Find the area of the largest square.

b. Find the length of the longest side
of the triangle.

Reaching All Learners

Intervention

In problem 13, because several steps are necessary, some students may need
prompting. You could ask, *What is the area of each of the smaller squares?
What is the area of the largest square? How can you find the length of one
side?* Students may need to look at their gray or white squares and be
reminded that a square with an area of 100 has a side length of 10. They
may guess and check to find the side length if the area is 169. Some
students may need the help of a calculator.

Solutions and Samples

12. The area is 52 cm^2.

Sample calculations:

$6^2 = 36$ cm^2; $4^2 = 16$ cm^2

36 cm^2 + 16 cm^2 = 52 cm^2

13. a. 25 cm^2 + 144 cm^2 = 169 cm^2

    b. The area of the square is 169 cm^2, so a side is 13 cm. Students may use different explanations how they arrived at 13.

       Because 13 × 13 = 169.

       Because $\sqrt{169}$ = 13.

Hints and Comments

Overview

Students start to use the Pythagorean theorem to find side lengths of right triangles.

About the Mathematics

On this page, the Pythagorean theorem is not formally stated as $a^2 + b^2 = c^2$ but is presented using area language. To help students develop insight into the possible application of this theorem, use area language frequently. Students should understand at this point that this theorem applies only to right triangles.

Planning

You may discuss the text on this page with the whole class before students start to work on problems 12 and 13. Problem 13 can be used as Informal Assessment.

Comments About the Solutions

13. This problem assesses students' ability to use the Pythagorean theorem using area language.

If students do not remember that they can use the square root key on their calculator, they can find the length of the side using guess and check:

.... × .... = 169

Notes

You can find the length of the sides of a square by "unsquaring" the area; for example:

The length of the sides of this square is the **square root** of 5.

The square root of 5 is written $\sqrt{5}$.

You can use a calculator to estimate the length for the square root of 5.

$\sqrt{5} \approx 2.24$

Therefore, each side of the square is about 2.24 cm.

14a It is a good idea to have students estimate the square root first by thinking what number times itself is about 52. Looking at their gray and white squares may be necessary for some.

14a Point out that when students do not have a calculator available, they can write the side length using the square root symbol: $\sqrt{52}$

the length of the side = $\sqrt{52}$.

Note that here the = sign is used because $\sqrt{52}$ is an exact answer.

14. **a.** Look back at the white square in problem 12. Use the square root notation to show the length of the side of the square.

   b. Use your calculator to approximate the length of the sides of the white square. Round your answer to one decimal place.

This figure shows a right triangle with short sides of 3 cm and 5 cm. There are many ways to find the length of side *AB*.

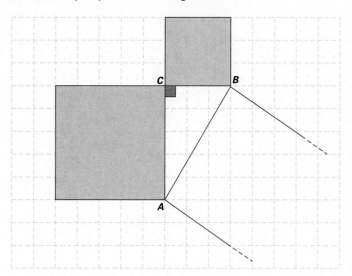

Reaching All Learners

Intervention

If finding the square root is new for some students, it is probably a good idea to have them first look at their gray or white squares and find the square root of numbers such as 16, 25, or 36 (perfect squares). Then reinforce that the square root of 4 is 2 because $2 \times 2 = 4$ and the square root of 5 is 2.24 because 2.24×2.24 is about 5.

Solutions and Samples

14. a. The side length is $\sqrt{52}$ cm.

   b. $\sqrt{52} \approx 7.2$, so the side lengths of the square are about 7.2 cm.

Hints and Comments

Materials

calculator (one per student)

Overview

On this page the relationship between the area and the side length of a square is reviewed. Students use the square root to find an estimate for side length of squares.

Planning

When students finish problem 14, you may discuss their answers. Also involve the rules for rounding in this discussion. For example, ask students to explain how to round the following numbers to one decimal.

7.152 [$\approx$ 7.2]   8.649 [$\approx$ 8.6]

4.872 [$\approx$ 4.9]   5.972 [$\approx$ 6.0]

The $\approx$ sign can be used to indicate that the answer is not an exact answer.

Sides and Angles

Notes

15 An organized way for students to write their calculation is the boxed solution strategy. Encourage students to use this notation.

Here is one way to find the length of side *AB*.

> area of the square on side *AC* = ...
>
> area of the square on side *BC* = ...
>
> $+$
>
> ....
>
> area of the square on side *AB* = ...
>
> so *AB* = ...

15. Find the length of side *AB*. Round your answer to the nearest tenth.

Here are two right triangles.

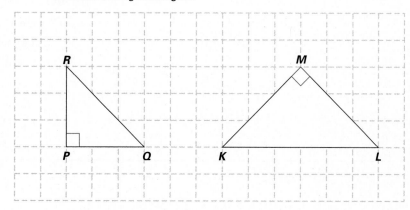

16a Encourage students to show their calculations as done in the previous example. First list the area of the square on side *PR*, then the area of a square on side *PQ*. Add these to get the area of a square of side *RQ*. Last find the square root to get the length of side *RQ*.

16a and **16b** You may want to have a discussion about the similarities and differences in these two triangles before they begin their work.

16. a. Find the side lengths of △*PQR*. Show your work.

b. Find the side lengths of △*KLM*. Show your work.

Assessment Pyramid

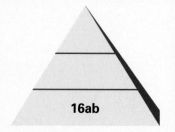

16ab

Use properties of triangles.

Reaching All Learners

Intervention

Some students may not realize that the diagonal is not one when the side length is one, so they may need to measure or discuss why the diagonal is longer than one. This problem requires them to work backwards. They know the length of the hypotenuse and must find the lengths of the two equal sides. It may be helpful to have students list what information they do know about △*KLM*. Looking back at problem 8 in this section may also help. Drawing the two squares on sides *KM* and *LM* that have a combined area of 36 should enable them to find the area of one of the squares and then the square root.

Solutions and Samples

15. area of the square on $AC =$ 25 cm²
area of the square on $BC =$ 9 cm²

      ⎯⎯⎯⎯⎯⎯⎯⎯
                     34 cm²

area of the square on $AB = 34$ cm²
so $AB = \sqrt{34} \approx 5.8$ cm.

16. a. $PQ = 3$ cm, $PR = 3$ cm, and $RQ = \sqrt{18} \approx 4.2$ cm.

Sample calculation for side RQ:

area of the square on $PQ =$ 9 cm²
area of the square on $PR =$ 9 cm²

      ⎯⎯⎯⎯⎯⎯⎯⎯
                     18 cm²

area of the square on $RQ = 18$ cm²
so $RQ = \sqrt{18} \approx 4.2$ cm.

b. $KL = 6$ cm, $LM = KM = \sqrt{18} \approx 4.2$ cm

Sample calculation for LM and KM:

area of the square on $KL = 36$ cm²

$\triangle KLM$ is an isosceles triangle, so the square on KM is equal to the square on LM.

Together they are 36 cm², so each square has an area of 18 cm².

The side lengths of the squares is $\sqrt{18} \approx 4.2$ cm.

Hints and Comments

Materials

calculator (one per student)

Overview

Students use the Pythagorean theorem to find side lengths of right triangles.

Planning

Students can work on problems 15 and 16 individually. You may have a discussion of students' answers on problem 15 before they continue with problem 16. Problem 16 can be used as Informal Assessment or as homework.

Comments About the Solutions

15. An alternative notation is:

Side Length	Area
$AC = 5$	25
$BC = 3$	+ 9
$AB = ?$	34

It is important that the largest side, and thus the largest area, is filled at the bottom of the diagram.

16. This problem demonstrates students' ability to use the Pythagorean theorem.

Notes

To get the students actively involved in reviewing the Summary, they could work with a partner, with one student writing the kind of triangle and the other one drawing the example. In addition, they could explain the Pythagorean theorem to each other.

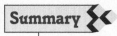

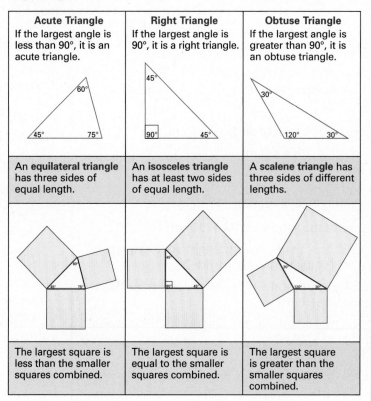

Triangles are classified into three types according to the size of the largest angle.

Acute Triangle	Right Triangle	Obtuse Triangle
If the largest angle is less than 90°, it is an acute triangle.	If the largest angle is 90°, it is a right triangle.	If the largest angle is greater than 90°, it is an obtuse triangle.
An **equilateral triangle** has three sides of equal length.	An **isosceles triangle** has at least two sides of equal length.	A **scalene triangle** has three sides of different lengths.
The largest square is less than the smaller squares combined.	The largest square is equal to the smaller squares combined.	The largest square is greater than the smaller squares combined.

Reaching All Learners

Extension

You may have students make up two problems that can be solved using the Pythagorean theorem. One should be an easy one, and one should be difficult to solve. They should provide solutions to their problems.
Then they exchange problems with a classmate, and they solve each others' problem.

Hints and Comments

Overview

Students read the Summary, which reviews the main concepts covered in this section.

Notes

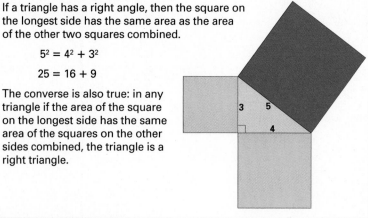

The Pythagorean Theorem

If a triangle has a right angle, then the square on the longest side has the same area as the area of the other two squares combined.

$$5^2 = 4^2 + 3^2$$

$$25 = 16 + 9$$

The converse is also true: in any triangle if the area of the square on the longest side has the same area of the squares on the other sides combined, the triangle is a right triangle.

Check Your Work

1 If students no longer have their pictures, they could just draw a triangle.

1. **a.** Choose any triangle from the pictures you collected at the beginning of this unit. Label the largest angle and the smallest angle. Justify your answer using only a ruler.

   b. Choose another triangle and label the longest side and the shortest side. Justify your answer using only a compass card or a protractor.

2. Classify the triangle formed by the three squares. Explain your reasoning.

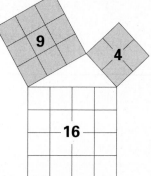

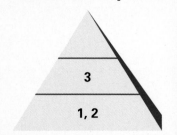

Assessment Pyramid

3

1, 2

Assesses Section D Goals

Reaching All Learners

Intervention

For problem 2, prompt students to review their poster if they have difficulty with the explanation.

Solutions and Samples

Answers to Check Your Work

1. **a.** and **b.**
   Share your findings with a classmate and discuss your work.

2. This is an obtuse triangle because the area of the white square (16 cm²) is greater than the area of the two gray squares (9 cm² and 4 cm² combined is 13 cm²).

Hints and Comments

Materials

centimeter ruler (one per student);
compass card or protractor (one per student)

Check Your Work Problems

These problems are designed for student self-assessment. A student who can answer the questions correctly has understood enough of the concepts taught in the section to be able to start the next section. Students who have difficulties in answering the questions without help may need extra practice.

This section is also useful for parents who want to help their children with their work.

Answers are provided in the Student Book. Have students discuss their answers with classmates.

After students complete Section D, you may assign appropriate activities from the Additional Practice section, located on page 57 of the *Triangles and Beyond* Student Book, for homework.

Comments About the Solutions

1. You may ask students to describe the strategies they used.

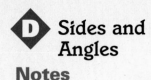

3. Use two different strategies to show that the area of the white square is 32 cm².

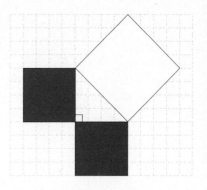

4. **a.** Find the lengths of the sides of △*PQR*. Show your work.

   b. Find the lengths of the sides of △*KLM*. Show your work.

4 You may wish to encourage students to use a drawing on graph paper for their explanations.

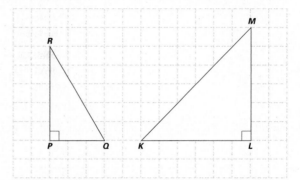

For Further Reflection

You can classify a triangle such as a scalene right triangle. Using length classifications of isosceles, scalene, and equilateral together with angle classifications of right, acute, and obtuse, tell which pairs are possible and which are impossible. Explain the reasons for your answers.

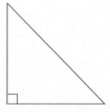

Assessment Pyramid

4, ☐FFR

Assesses Section D Goals

Reaching All Learners

Intervention

Drawing the squares on the sides of the triangle helps many students avoid the common error of squaring 3 and getting 6. From the square they can see it must be 9.

Extension

Students could construct all the triangles that are possible, such as right isosceles triangle, and label each with the correct vocabulary.

Accommodation

For problem 4, some students might need a copy of this page so they can draw lines inside the white square.

34   **Triangles and Beyond**

Solutions and Samples

3. One strategy applies the Pythagorean theorem: The sum of the area of the gray squares is $(16 \text{ cm}^2 + 16 \text{ cm}^2) = 32 \text{ cm}^2$, so the area of the white square is 32 cm^2.

Another strategy uses reallotment.

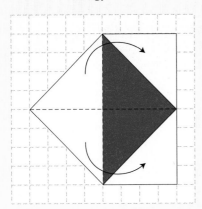

Two triangular pieces from the square are reallotted into a 4 x 8 rectangle. The area of this rectangle is 32 cm^2.

4. a. $PQ = 3$ cm and $PR = 5$ cm.
area of the square on $PQ =$ 9 cm²
area of the square on $\underline{PR = 25 \text{ cm}^2}$
                                              34 cm²
area of the square on $QR = 34 \text{ cm}^2$,
so $RQ = \sqrt{34} \text{ cm}^2$.

b. $KL = 6$ cm and $LM = 6$ cm.
area of the square on $KL = 36 \text{ cm}^2$
area of the square on $\underline{LM = 36 \text{ cm}^2}$
                                              72 cm²
area of the square on $KM = 72 \text{ cm}^2$,
so $KM = \sqrt{72} \approx 8.5$ cm.

For Further Reflection

There are nine combinations that have to be checked:
- isosceles – right   is possible, it is half a square
- isosceles – acute   is possible
- isosceles – obtuse   is possible

Sample explanation:

I can draw them:

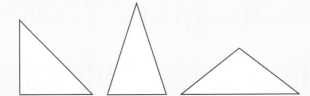

Hints and Comments

Materials

graph paper (one sheet per student);
calculator (optional, one per student)
copy of Student Book page 34 (optional)

Comments About the Solutions

4. Students can give an exact answer using the square root sign, or an estimate using a calculator.

- scalene – right   is possible
- scalene – acute   is possible
- scalene – obtuse   is possible

Sample explanation:

3 cm, 4 cm, 5 cm is a scalene right triangle. It is a right triangle because I checked with the Pythagorean theorem.

If I make the largest side of 5 cm larger, I will get an obtuse triangle; for example, 3 cm, 4 cm, and 6 cm.

If I make the largest side shorter, but larger than 4 cm, I will get an acute triangle; for example, 3 cm, 4 cm, 4.5 cm.

- equilateral – right   is not possible
- equilateral – acute   is possible
- equilateral – obtuse   is not possible

Explanation: An equilateral triangle has three equal angles of 60°, so it is always an acute triangle.

Section Focus

Students learn how shapes can be flipped, turned, or slid to create a desired effect. In this way they are introduced to the transformations reflection, rotation, and translation. They are introduced to the concept of congruent figures. They start to investigate the properties of the corresponding side length and angle measurements of two congruent figures. Students look for symmetry in shapes and for lines of symmetry. The instructional focus of Section E is to:

- solve problems involving translations, rotations, and reflections;
- identify congruent figures; and
- identify a line of symmetry.

Pacing and Planning

Day 13: Stamps and Stencils		Student pages 35–38
INTRODUCTION	Problem 1	Investigate translations, rotations, and reflections in a simple drawing.
ACTIVITY	Activity: Stencil Design	Investigate reflections and rotations by folding paper and making cutouts.
CLASSWORK	Problems 2–5	Use the terms congruent, translation, rotation, and reflection to describe various figures.
HOMEWORK	Activity: Stencils Transformed	Solve problems involving translations, rotations, and reflections.

Day 14: Line Symmetry		Student pages 39–41
INTRODUCTION	Problem 6	Identify line of symmetry in a drawing.
CLASSWORK	Problems 7–9; For Further Reflection	Solve problems involving lines of symmetry.
HOMEWORK	Check Your Work	Student self-assessment: Demonstrate translations, rotations, and reflections; identify and describe lines of symmetry.

Day 15: Summary		
REVIEW	Sections A–E review	Review summary pages and geometric properties from Sections A through E.
ASSESSMENT	Quiz #2	Assesses Section A through E goals.

Additional Resources: Additional Practice Section E, page 58

Materials

Student Resources
No resources required.

Teachers Resources
No resources required.

Student Materials
Quantities listed are per pair of students, unless otherwise noted.

- Drawing paper (one per student)
- Scissors

* See Hints and Comments for optional materials.

Learning Lines

Concepts: Congruency, and Transformations

The context of making copies using stamps and stencils is used to introduce the concept of congruency. At this stage students start to work with an informal description of the concept of congruent figures: figures that are copies of each other. Congruent figures have the same size and shape; they can fit on top of each other exactly with no overlap.

In order to see if two figures are congruent, one of the figures can be moved around until it fits on the other one. Students learn to describe these movements (transformations) using formal language: translation, rotation, and reflection.

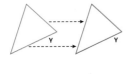

In Section F, translations are combined to construct regular polygons, parallelograms, and rectangles.

At the End of This Section

Students can solve problems involving translations, rotations, and reflections. They can identify congruent figures. They understand and can identify line symmetry and line of reflection.

Congruent Triangles

Stamps and Stencils

1 Discuss the difference between a stamp and a stencil. If possible, show them some stamps and stencils.

1c Students may describe all possibilities in terms of monkey **a**. If students say only which side of the stencil is used, encourage them to make their descriptions more precise.

Mark buys a set of monkey stamps at a toy store for his younger sister Mia. She uses her stamp set to make this design.

1. a. What is the minimum number of stamps Mia needs to make the design? Explain your answer.

   b. The toy store also sells animal stencils. If Mia purchases stencils instead of stamps, how many stencils does she need to make her design?

   c. Explain how to use the stencil to draw each monkey in Mia's design.

Reaching All Learners

Intervention

Some students may need a copy of the monkeys and cut them apart so it is easier to compare them. The cut-out is like the stamp—it cannot be turned over. Save the shapes for doing problem 4a on page 37.

Extension

You may ask students to bring their own stencils to class. Then they may investigate these stencils to see whether or not the picture is different when the stencil is flipped. (For some stencils, it may not make a difference if it is flipped.)

Solutions and Samples

1. **a.** Mia needs two stamps because there are two different monkeys, one with the tail pointing left and one with the tail pointing right. The monkeys are reflections of each other. Because a stamp cannot be flipped, she needs two different stamps.

   b. She needs only one stencil because a stencil can be flipped, or turned over, to create a reflection of the original monkey.

   c. Answers may vary. Sample response:

   Monkey **a** can be drawn using this side of the stencil.

   Monkey **b** is a rotation of **a**, so this side of the stencil still works.

   Monkey **c** requires a flip of the stencil and a rotation.

   Monkey **d** is a flip of **c**, so we must go back to the original side of the stencil.

   Monkey **e** is a flip of **d**, so we must use the other side of the stencil.

   In short, **a**, **b**, and **d** can be made with one side of the stencil, and **c** and **e** with the other side.

Hints and Comments

Materials
Copies of monkey (optional)

Overview
Students investigate making pictures using a stamp and a stencil. They discover that a stencil has the advantage that it can be flipped over to create a reflection. In this context, students start to see how flips, turns, and slides affect pictures.

About the Mathematics
This section informally introduces the three transformations: reflection (flip over), rotation (turn), and translation (slide).

Planning
When students finish problem 1, you may want to discuss the answers with them. Students may work on this problem individually.

Comments About the Solutions

1. It is important that students use their own words in answering this problem. Formal terminology will be introduced on Student Book page 37. Students' answers should mention all three transformations: flips, slides, and turns.

Notes

Activity

Advise students to make a shape that is not too difficult to cut out and that is not symmetric. Many students enjoy doing their name initial.

It is important that students cut out an irregular shape (the shape of a hand works well); otherwise they may not see the different transformations.

You may wish to use a mirror to show why certain images are called reflections, or mirror images.

Encourage students to use expressions such as *flip*, *turn*, and *slide*.

Activity

Stencil Design

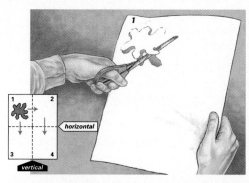

- Fold the paper in half vertically and then horizontally. Unfold your paper. Cut out an irregular shape in the top left corner of a sheet of paper. Write the number 1 in the corner near the cutout.

- Fold the paper in half vertically. Then use the hole as a stencil and trace the shape on the right side of the paper.

- Unfold the paper and cut out your new shape. Write the number 2 near the new cutout.

In your notebook, describe the relationship between the two cutouts.

- Fold your paper in half horizontally and trace shapes 1 and 2 onto the bottom of the page. Write the number 3 in the lower left corner and the number 4 in the lower right corner.

In your notebook, describe the relationship between shapes 2 and 3.

Describe the relationship between shapes 1 and 4. Why do you think this happened?

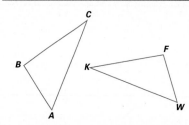

Figures that are copies of each other are called **congruent figures**. Congruent figures have the same size and shape. Using the concepts of translation, rotation and reflection, a copy of one figure can fit exactly on top of the other figure.

2. Are △ *ABC* and △ *WFK* congruent? Explain how you know for sure.

Reaching All Learners

Vocabulary Building

Add the term *congruent* to your vocabulary poster.

Extension

Students could use a marker or pen to go over the fold line ,so when they do problem 4b on page 37, they can see the line of symmetry. Students enjoy seeing their designs posted on the classroom wall.

Solutions and Samples

Activity

Sample responses:

- Shapes 1 and 2

  The two cutouts are mirror images of each other. The second shape is the first one flipped over the vertical line.

- Shapes 2 and 3

  The third shape is the second shape turned (half a turn, or rotated 180°), or

  The two shapes are rotations (turns) of each other.

- Shapes 1 and 4

  The fourth shape is the first shape turned (half a turn, or rotated 180°), or

  The two shapes are rotations (turns) of each other.

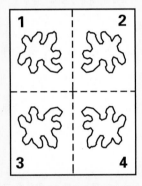

2. Yes, they are congruent. Explanations will vary. Students may trace one of the shapes and cut out the figure. They can then place it on top of the other shape. Students may also measure sides and angles to compare the triangles.

Hints and Comments

Materials

drawing paper (one sheet per student);
scissors (one pair per student);
tracing paper (optional, one sheet per student)

Overview

Students make a stencil and use this stencil to make a variety of new images by folding and tracing the original shape. Then they look for relationships between the shapes they have made.
Then students learn the concept of congruent figures.

Planning

Have students work on the activity in small groups. Have a class discussion about students' answers when students have finished the activity and answered the questions that are in the activity.

When students finish problem 4, you may wish to discuss the concept of congruent figures. Ask students to explain in their own words how they can tell whether two figures are congruent.

Comments About the Activity

If the folds are perpendicular, this will work. If the folds are not perpendicular, the images cannot be superimposed exactly. This is investigated on Student Book page 38.

E Congruent Triangles

Notes

Ask students to explain in their own words how they can tell whether two figures are congruent. Then discuss the text on this page.

3b and 3c It may be helpful to have an informal discussion of what we mean by *corresponding angles* and *corresponding sides* when describing the relationship between the angles and sides of each figure.

4 You may want to use two triangles and an overhead projector to show the movements and introduce their formal names.

3. **a.** Construct two new congruent figures. Describe how you created your shapes.

   b. Describe the relationships between the angles of each figure.

   c. Describe the relationships between the side lengths of each figure.

Transformations

You can move figures around to determine if they are congruent. These movements are called **transformations**. There are three special types of transformations.

Translation—sliding a figure so that each point moves the same distance in the same direction.

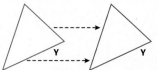

Triangle Y has been translated to the right.

Rotation—turning a figure around a point along a circular path.

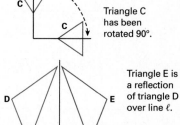

Triangle C has been rotated 90°.

Reflection—making a mirror image of a figure by flipping it over a line. This line is called the **line of reflection**.

Triangle E is a reflection of triangle D over line ℓ.

4. **a.** Look at Mia's design on page 35. Select two monkeys from Mia's design and describe the transformation(s) (translation, rotation, and/or reflection) needed to move one monkey directly on top of the other. Repeat this problem with another pair of monkeys.

   b. Refer to the Stencil Design Activity on page 36. Describe the transformation(s) you used to create the copies. Describe other transformations that can be used to make the copies.

Reaching All Learners

Hands-On Learning

Kinesthetic activities are good for reinforcing the vocabulary words— *translation, rotation,* and *reflection.* Have students demonstrate translation (slide), rotation (spin or turn), and reflection (flip) with their bodies.

Extension

It is interesting to look at flags from various countries and see what transformations can be used to make them or have the students design a flag and describe the transformations used to create it.

Solutions and Samples

3. a. Answers may vary. Sample answer:

I folded a piece of paper and cut out a shape, so I got it double.

b. Sample responses:

For each angle of one shape, I can find a same angle in the other shape, or

The angles are the same.

c. For each side length of one shape, I can find a same side length in the other shape, or

The side lengths are the same.

4. a. Answers will vary. Rotations, reflections, and translations are all used in these figures. Sample responses:

Monkey A to monkey B: rotate and translate.

Monkey A to monkey C: reflect, rotate, and translate.

Monkey A to monkey D: translate and rotate.

Monkey A to monkey E: reflect, rotate, and translate.

b. Shapes 2 and 3 are reflections of shape 1. Shapes 2 and 3 are rotations of one another. Shape 4 is a reflection of shape 2 (and of shape 3, as well, if the folds were made perfectly perpendicular). Shape 4 is a rotation of shape 1.

Hints and Comments

Materials

congruent triangles (optional, two per class); overhead projector (optional, one per class)

Overview

Students further investigate the concept of congruent figures. Then they learn the mathematical expressions for turns, flips, and slides and use these new terms in descriptions.

About the Mathematics

A *translation* is a movement of a figure in a certain direction over a certain distance. This movement can be indicated by a vector.

A *rotation* is the result of turning a figure around a particular point. This point is called the *center of rotation*.

A *reflection* is the result of flipping a figure over a line. This line is called the *line of reflection*.

Planning

When students finish problem 3, you may wish to discuss the concept of congruent figures. Students may work on problem 4 individually.

Notes

These designs were created by moving one triangle to a new location and then changing colors.

Design A   Design B

5. For each new design, pick a starting triangle and use the terms *translation, rotation,* and *reflection* to describe the movements used to make the design. Include coloring in your description.

5 Discuss various student solutions and ask if a reflection of an equilateral triangle can always be replaced by a rotation.

In the Stencil Design Activity on page 36, you made two reflections of an irregular shape over two perpendicular lines. You folded the paper along lines of reflection. You saw that these two reflections have the same result as rotating the original shape half a turn (180°).

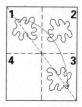

 Activity

Activity

The reflection over non-perpendicular lines and parallel lines is optional. If time permits, you might have some students do the reflections over non-perpendicular lines and others do the reflections over parallel lines and share their results.

Stencils Transformed

For this activity, you will need some paper and scissors.

* Investigate what happens when you reflect an irregular shape over two lines that are not perpendicular. Use cutting and folding to discover what happens. Is the resulting image still a rotation of the original shape?

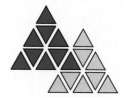

* Investigate what happens if the two lines of reflection are parallel.

* Summarize your investigations. Be very precise in describing any rotation.

Assessment Pyramid

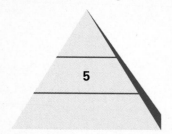

Describe transformations using words and diagrams.

Reaching All Learners

Intervention

For problem 5, some students may need a copy of an equilateral triangle to manipulate in order to analyze the transformations. Pattern blocks can be used. Students will see how a reflection of an equilateral triangle produces the same result as a rotation.

Vocabulary Building

Some students may need a review of the term *perpendicular* for discussing the two reflections over two perpendicular lines. Add *perpendicular* to your glossary.

Solutions and Samples

5. Answers will vary. Sample responses:

For design A, start with the upper left triangle and rotate it about its yellow vertex. Repeat three more times and change the coloring. Design A also could be made by reflecting one triangle over several lines as shown below.

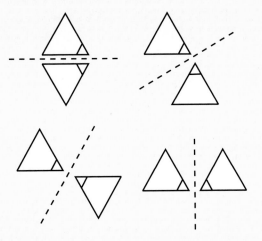

Design B can be created by reflecting triangles after starting with one. The design can also be made by translating larger groups of triangles.

Activity

• Yes, the resulting image is still a rotation.

• Answers may vary. Students may note that in this case, the two reflections cannot be replaced by one rotation. They can be replaced by a translation as shown below:

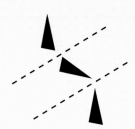

Hints and Comments

Materials

drawing paper (one sheet per student); scissors (one pair per student)

Overview

Students investigate designs that can be made by translating, rotating, and/or reflecting one figure. Students investigate whether or not two reflections can always be replaced by a rotation.

About the Mathematics

When a figure is reflected twice across intersecting lines, the result is the same as a rotation of the original figure. (And, actually, the angle of rotation is double the angle between the lines of reflection.) When a figure is reflected twice across parallel lines, the result is the same as a translation of the original figure (and the distance of the translation is twice the distance between the lines). Do not expect students to discover the specific measurement relationship. An even number of reflections will produce the original figure, and an odd number of reflections will produce a mirror image of the original figure.

Planning

Discuss students' descriptions for problem 5. Problem 5 may be assigned as homework.

Comments About the Solutions

5. This problem may be assigned as homework.

Activity

Some students may have used a reflection; others may have used a rotation for the same situation. This may lead to the statement that a reflection of an equilateral triangle can be replaced by a rotation and vice versa.

If time is a concern, you may omit this problem or assign it as homework. Alternatively, you may want to divide the class into two groups, with one group working with two lines of reflection that are not perpendicular and the other with two lines of reflection that are parallel. Then have the two groups exchange their results.

Extension

Students could check to see if a reflection and a rotation produce the same result for other kinds of triangles.

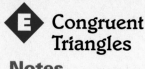
E Congruent Triangles

Notes

7 Students enjoy using small mirrors to check symmetry.

8 You may want to have students cut out their triangles and verify the lines of symmetry by folding.

9 The designs could be done on graph paper and colored paper. Students can exchange designs to check for lines of symmetry.

All students should be able to design a figure with one line of symmetry. If students find this difficult, you may want to remind them that the folding line is the line of symmetry. Using graph paper may also be helpful.

Line Symmetry

6. Copy the two triangles below. Use the dotted lines to create a reflection of each shape. What is the difference in the resulting image?

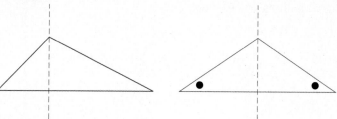

If a figure contains a line of reflection, it has **line symmetry**. Some symmetrical shapes have more than one **line of symmetry**, as shown in the figure on the right.

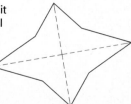

ABCDEFGHIJKLM NOPQRSTUVWXYZ

7. **a.** Which capital letters have line symmetry?

   b. Which capital letters have more than one line of symmetry?

8. If possible, design three triangles, each with one of the following characteristics:

   a. one line of symmetry

   b. two lines of symmetry

   c. three lines of symmetry

9. Create a design that has one or more lines of symmetry.

Assessment Pyramid

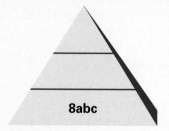

8abc

Understand and identify line symmetry.

Reaching All Learners

Intervention

Be sure students understand the definition of *line symmetry*. Have some shapes, such as a regular hexagon, made out of paper to fold and demonstrate line symmetry. (Both parts of the figure should cover each other perfectly.)

Extension

Students could look for examples of line symmetry in nature (animals, insects, plants, etc.) and bring a sample, such as a leaf, to class, or they could make a sketch that shows the line of symmetry.

Solutions and Samples

6. For the second triangle the resulting image coincides with the original triangle.

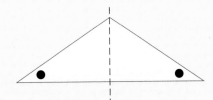

For the first triangle this is not the case.

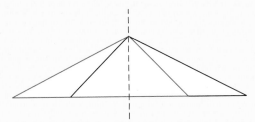

7. a. A, B, C, D, E, H, I, M, O, T, U, V, W, X, and Y have line symmetry.

b. H, I, O, and X have more than one line of symmetry.

8. a. An isosceles triangle that is not an equilateral triangle has exactly one line of symmetry.

b. No triangle has exactly two lines of symmetry.

c. An equilateral triangle has three lines of symmetry:

9. Designs will vary.

Hints and Comments

Materials

tracing paper and graph paper (optional, one sheet per student);
hand-held mirror (optional, one per class)

Overview

Students identify symmetry in figures and look for one or more lines of symmetry in these figures. They also create figures with one or more lines of symmetry.

About the Mathematics

A figure that contains a line of reflection has line symmetry. This means that if you connect any two matching points, the line of symmetry would be the perpendicular bisector of the segment drawn.

Planning

Before students continue, you may want to discuss problem 6 to check that they understand the concept of line symmetry. Have students work individually on problems 7–9. Problem 7 may be used as an informal assessment.

Comments About the Solutions

6. The reflection of the first triangle may be difficult for students to draw. They can trace the triangle and the line of reflection and then flip the tracing paper so the line of reflection fits to the original.

9. To solve this problem, students must be able to recognize line symmetry, create a symmetrical figure, explain why it is symmetrical, and test that symmetry.

Congruent
Triangles

Notes

This would be a good opportunity to have students review the properties learned so far in this unit.

Have students reread the Summary for Sections A through E as review before taking Quiz 2.

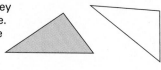 Summary

Two figures are congruent when they are exactly the same size and shape. Corresponding angles are the same size. Corresponding sides are the same lengths.

Transformations are used to create congruent shapes.

When you slide a figure so each point moves the same distance in the same direction, it is called a translation.

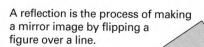

A rotation means that a figure is turned around a point along a circular path.

A reflection is the process of making a mirror image by flipping a figure over a line.

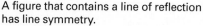

A figure that contains a line of reflection has line symmetry.

If a figure is translated, rotated, or reflected, the resulting figure is congruent to the original figure.

Reaching All Learners

Vocabulary Building

Some students may benefit from making vocabulary cards out of index cards with the definition and visual clue on the back. Review games could be played using the cards and small marker boards.

Hints and Comments

Overview

Students read the Summary, which describes the terms *congruent, translation, rotation, reflection,* and *line symmetry.*

Congruent Triangles

Notes

1 Allow students the option of cutting out their figure and tracing it if necessary.

2 You may want to discuss the difference between a drawing of a three-dimensional object and the three-dimensional object itself with respect to line symmetry. If in the drawing, which is two dimensional, you can draw a *line of symmetry*, the actual shape has a *plane of symmetry*.

4 Some students may need a paper copy of a rectangle and square to fold and check. A sheet of notebook paper would work for the rectangle and another sheet could be folded and cut to make a square.

 Check Your Work

1. Draw a figure and show three transformations: translation, reflection, and rotation.

2. Write a few sentences describing what it means for something to be symmetrical. Include examples of symmetrical objects.

3. Which of these letters can be rotated 180° and still look the same?

ABCDEFGHIJKLM
NOPQRSTUVWXYZ

4. In your notebook, draw a rectangle and a square and draw their lines of symmetry. How are their lines of symmetry different? How are they the same?

For Further Reflection

Consider the squares you used in the Making Triangles from Squares activity on page 25. How many lines of symmetry are in each square? Describe the areas of each part of the square after you have drawn the lines of symmetry.

Assessment Pyramid

2, 3, 4, ◻FFR

Assesses Section E Goals

Reaching All Learners

Extension

If your students have completed the unit *Operations*, you can have them draw a polygon on a coordinate grid, label the vertices with the coordinates, and then do various transformations. They could also identify the coordinates of the transformed figure.

Solutions and Samples

Answers to Check Your Work

1. Here is one possible transformation showing a translation, then a rotation and a reflection of a pentagon:

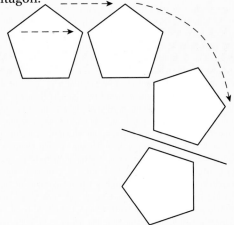

2. Here is one possible description:

   For anything to be symmetrical, there has to be at least one line of symmetry. A line of symmetry splits an object in half so that if you could fold the object along this line, each side would match up perfectly.

   Put a mirror along the line of symmetry and see if the original part and the reflected part are the same.

   Many everyday objects are symmetrical. For example, the fork and a spoon pictured here have one line of symmetry each.

   A cup with a handle has only one line of symmetry, while a cup without a handle has many lines of symmetry, as shown here.

   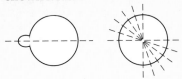

3. The letters H, I, N, O, S, X, and Z look the same when they are rotated 180°. (Note: Turn the page upside down to see which letters look the same.)

4. As shown below, a rectangle has two lines of symmetry and a square has four lines of symmetry.

Hints and Comments

Check Your Work Problems

These problems are designed for student self-assessment. A student who can answer the questions correctly has understood enough of the concepts taught in the section to be able to start the next section. Students who have difficulties in answering the questions without help may need extra practice.

This section is also useful for parents who want to help their children with their work.

Answers are provided in the Student Book. Have students discuss their answers with classmates.

After students complete Section E, you may assign for homework appropriate activities from the Additional Practice section, located on page 58 of the *Triangles and Beyond* Student Book.

Comments About the Solutions

3. Note that letters that can be rotated over 180° and still look the same can easily be found by turning the book 180°. So you can read these letters upside down.

4. The square and rectangle have both a horizontal and vertical line of symmetry; however, many students think that the diagonal of a rectangle is also a line of symmetry.

For Further Reflection

Any square has four lines of symmetry. The area of each part of the square divided by these lines of symmetry is one-eighth of the total area.

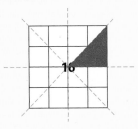

So for this square, which has an area of 16 square units, the area of each part is 2 square units (This can also be verified visually, by reallotting the triangular pieces, or using the formula for the area of a triangle.)

Section Focus

Students construct parallel lines and families of parallel lines using a straightedge and a plastic triangle. They construct parallelograms using strips and learn to identify different types of parallelograms (rectangle, rhombus, square). Students construct regular polygons, parallelograms, and rectangles by rotating and translating triangles. The instructional focus of Section F is to:

- draw parallel lines using a straightedge and a cardboard triangle;
- solve problems involving parallel lines;
- identify and describe parallelograms, rectangles, rhombi, and squares; and
- Describe the relationship between polygons and their central angles.

Pacing and Planning

Day 16: Constructing Parallel Lines		Student pages 42–46
ACTIVITY	Activity: Constructing Parallel Lines	Draw parallel lines using a straightedge and a cardboard triangle.
CLASSWORK	Problems 1 – 4	Solve problems involving parallel lines and angles formed by lines that intersect parallel lines.
ACTIVITY	Activity: Parallelograms Problems 5 and 6	Construct a set of parallelograms and describe their similarities and differences.
HOMEWORK	Problem 7	Identify parallelograms from a set of quadrilaterals.

Day 17: Parallelograms		Student pages 47–49
INTRODUCTION	Problem 8–10	Describe the characteristics of various parallelograms.
ACTIVITY	Activity: Combining Transformations	Construct a set of parallelograms and describe their similarities and differences.
HOMEWORK	Problems 11 and 12	Describe how to use transformations to create polygons.

Day 18: Combining Transformations		Student pages 49–53
ACTIVITY	Activity: Rotating a Triangle	Rotate an isosceles triangle to create a new polygon.
CLASSWORK	Problems 13–15	Investigate the relationship between the central (vertex) angles and polygons.
HOMEWORK	Check Your Work; For Further Reflection	Student self-assessment: Identify and describe characteristics of quadrilaterals.

Additional Resources: Math History, page 51; Additional Practice Section F, pages 58 and 59

Materials

Student Resources
Quantities listed are per student.

• Student Activity Sheet 8

Teachers Resources
No resources required.

Student Materials
Quantities listed are per student, unless otherwise noted.

• Colored pencils two colors (per pair of students)
• Drawing paper
• Thick paper or index cards (per pair of students)
• Scissors
• Centimeter ruler
• Pair of compasses
• Protractor or compass card
• Straightedge
• Triangles, plastic or cardboard

* See Hints and Comments for optional materials.

Learning Lines

In this last section many topics studied in previous sections return and are combined.

Properties: Parallelograms

Students start to explore the properties of special parallelograms: a rectangle is a parallelogram with four equal angles that each measure 90°. A rhombus is a parallelogram with four equal sides, but not necessary four equal angles. A square is a parallelogram with four equal sides and four equal angles.

The characteristics of parallelograms are emphasized when they are constructed from a triangle and its image. This image is the result of a rotation of the original triangle around one of the vertices, followed by a translation.

Properties: Polygons

Polygons were introduced in the unit *Packages and Polygons*.

In this section, students make regular polygons by rotating a triangle with the correct vertex angle, which must be a factor of 360. (The concept of a factor is introduced in the unit *Facts and Factors*.) For example, 60 is a factor of 360. You can trace a triangle with a vertex angle of 60° and rotate it five times to create a hexagon.

 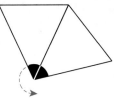

At the End of This Section

Students are able to construct parallel lines and families of parallel lines. Students can recognize and classify quadrilaterals (parallelogram, rectangle, rhombus, square). Students explore a way to construct regular polygons. Students solve problems involving translations, rotations, and reflections.

Activity

If plastic triangles are not available, you could make them with a paper cutter, or students could use scissors and cut various triangles. The triangles can be cut from card stock, used file folders, or foam board from a craft store.

vi If no one mentions that the lines are parallel because the lines form equal angles with the straightedge, ask them about the angles.

vi Some students may respond that they know the lines are parallel because the lines do not cross. If so, ask, *How can you be sure that the lines will never cross?* (They cannot cross because they were both drawn at the same angle to the straightedge.)

Activity

Constructing Parallel Lines

For this activity, you will need some paper, a straightedge or ruler, and a triangle template or one cutout from stiff cardboard.

In Section A, you studied families of parallel lines. Now you will learn how to construct "families" of parallel lines like a draftsperson or a designer.

  i. Use a straightedge to draw a straight line.

  ii. Place a plastic or cardboard triangle along the line that you drew. (A triangle of any shape will work.)

  iii. Place the straightedge against another side of the triangle.

  iv. While holding the straightedge still, slide the triangle along the straightedge.

  v. Draw a second line along the edge of your triangle that is parallel to the first line.

  vi. Repeat step **iv** and draw a third line, parallel to the first two lines.

  • How do you know that these three lines are parallel?

Reaching All Learners

Intervention

If students have difficulty, have them reconsider the answer to problem 7 of Section A.

Extension

If students cut a variety of triangles for this activity, they could also be used to review the vocabulary. One possibility is to sort the triangles according to angles (acute, right, obtuse) or sides (isosceles, equilateral, scalene).

Solutions and Samples

Activity

The three lines are parallel because the angles they make with the straightedge are equal (because it's the same angle in the triangle).

Hints and Comments

Materials

straightedge (one per student);
plastic or cardboard triangle (one per student)

Overview

Students learn how to draw parallel lines.

About the Mathematics

This activity involves the converse of what students investigated in Section A: parallel lines form equal angles with lines that intersect them; that is, if lines are constructed so that they form equal angles with a line intersecting them, the lines are parallel. Note that this is only true for lines in a two-dimensional situation, or in other words, if the lines are in the same plane. (In a three-dimensional situation, it is possible that two lines make the same angle with a third line without being parallel.)

Planning

Students may work on the activity in small groups.

Comments About the Solutions

This question can be used to guide students toward the idea of rigorous justification, which is an important part of mathematical reasoning.
These problems link parallelism to the concept of equal angles.

Triangles and Beyond

Notes

Start this page with a discussion of the difference between a top-view and a perspective drawing, such as the one pictured. It may help to have students model the rails with pencils or rulers before drawing.

1 Have students use colored pencils to indicate equal parts of the rails and equal angles. Note: the lines do not have to intersect at right angles.

1b Students should explain how they know which lines are equal and which angles are equal.

Here is a picture of some railroad tracks.

1. **a.** Make a top-view drawing of the six rails.

   b. In your drawing, mark the sections of the six rails that have the same lengths. Also mark the angles that have the same measures. You should not use a ruler or protractor to determine the measures.

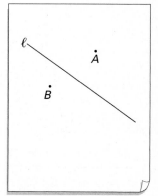

2. **a.** On a blank sheet of paper, draw a line and label it *l*. Draw two points, *A* and *B*, that are *not* on line *l*.

   b. Use a straightedge and your triangle from the activity on page 42. Draw a line through *A* that is parallel to line *l*. Label it *m*.

   c. Use your straightedge and triangle to draw a line through *B* that is parallel to line *l*. Label it *n*.

   d. Are lines m and n parallel? If they are, write *m // n*. The symbol // means *is parallel to*.

Now that you know how to draw one family of parallel lines, you are going to draw three families of parallel lines.

3. **a.** Draw three parallel lines like those shown on the right. Be sure that they are the same distance apart. This is the first family of parallel lines.

Reaching All Learners

Intervention

If students have difficulties with problem 2, ask them to first draw two parallel lines. Then ask them which instrument they moved and which they held in place. You may need to explain that they have to put one side of the triangle along line l, place the straightedge along another side of the triangle, and then slide the triangle along the edge of the straightedge until they reach point A.

Solutions and Samples

1. a.-b.

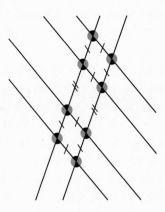

2. d. Yes, the lines are parallel, so $m \parallel n$.

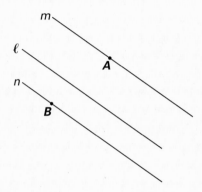

3. a. See page 44T.

Hints and Comments

Materials

centimeter ruler (one per student);
plastic or cardboard triangle (one per student);
colored pencils (optional, one box per student);
compass card or protractor (one per student)

Overview

Students make a top-view drawing of six rails and label equal line lengths and equal angles. Then they continue to draw parallel lines. They use a centimeter ruler instead of a straightedge. In Section A students investigated families of parallel lines. In problem 3 students start to draw three families of parallel lines.

Planning

Students may work on problems 1–3 in small groups. Problem 3 is continued on the next page.

Comments About the Solutions

1. The lines shown in the solutions column are equal because parallel lines are always the same distance apart. The angles are equal because parallel lines make equal angles with any line intersecting them.

3. **a.** If students use the centimeter ruler, they can draw parallel lines at equal distances.

Extension

You could discuss why the parallel rails in the picture appear to touch. Also ask them if they could think of any lines that never touch that are not parallel. Show them skew lines on a cube if they cannot think of an example.

b. Now draw a line that forms an angle of 20° with the horizontal lines.

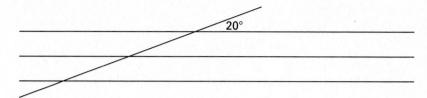

3c The distance between the parallel lines of the second family doesn't need to be the same as the distance between the parallel lines of the first family.

c. The new line is a member of the second family of parallel lines. Draw this family of parallel lines.

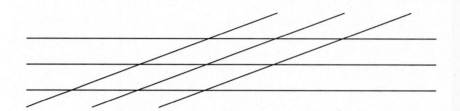

d. The intersections of these two families determine the third family. Draw a couple of members of this third family so you can find a triangular pattern.

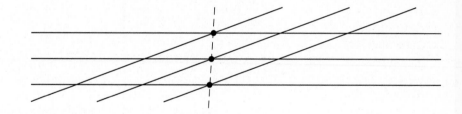

Reaching All Learners

English Language Learners

Some students may have difficulty with the word *relationships*. If this is the case, you could ask if any angles are the same size. If so, which angles are the same size?

Solutions and Samples

3. a.–d.

(Note that this drawing is reduced.)

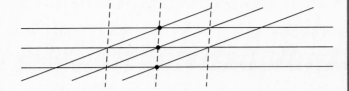

Hints and Comments

Materials

centimeter ruler (one per student);
plastic or cardboard triangle (one per student);
compass card or protractor (one per student)

Overview

Students draw three families of parallel lines that form a triangular grid.

Planning

Students continue working in small groups on problem 3. You may want to have them work individually on problem 4, because problem 4 can be used as informal assessment or assigned as homework. Discuss students' answers in class.

Comments About the Solutions

3. d. You may want to use the questions below to discuss the topic of transformation that students studied in the previous section.

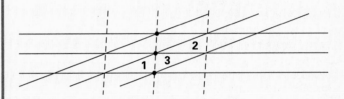

What transformation can be used to place triangle 1 on triangle 2? (A translation.) And on triangle 3? (A rotation.)

What transformation can be used to place triangle 2 on triangle 3? (A rotation.) Note that a reflection is not possible since the triangles are not isosceles triangles.

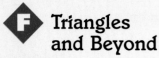

Triangles and Beyond

Notes

4a If students have trouble getting started, ask what the sum of the three equal angles in an equilateral triangle must be. Then they should be able to determine the measure of each angle in an equilateral triangle.

4b You might want them to make each family of parallel lines a separate color.

Be sure students know the only real requirement for a parallelogram is that it has four sides and the opposite sides are parallel. Discuss the other properties such as the fact that the opposite sides are the same length and opposite angles are congruent.

e. Describe any angle and triangle relationships in the triangular pattern.

f. Predict how the design will change if the angle used in part **b** changes.

4. a. Suppose you create three families of parallel lines so the triangles are equilateral triangles. Describe how to do this.

b. Check your answer by drawing a part of the triangular pattern.

Activity

Parallelograms

For this activity, you will need:

- paper;
- a transparency sheet;
- straightedge; and
- scissors.

i. Using a transparency, cut three long rectangular strips. One strip should be 2 cm wide and the other two strips should each be 3 cm wide.

ii. Place two strips across each other as shown in the drawing on the next page. Where the two strips overlap, a special **quadrilateral** is formed. This quadrilateral is called a **parallelogram**.

Assessment Pyramid

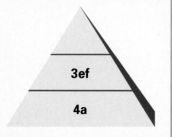

3ef

4a

Describe angle relationships when one line intersects parallel lines.

Create families of parallel lines.

Reaching All Learners

Accommodation

For the activity, if transparency sheets are not available, strips of card stock or poster paper will work.

Vocabulary Building

For part ii, add *parallelogram* to your vocabulary poster with several examples of parallelograms.

Solutions and Samples

3. e. The triangles in the pattern are scalene triangles. They are all congruent.

   f. In general, you will get the same pattern of triangles. But if you use, for example, an angle of 90°, then you will get a pattern of right triangles.

4. a. Change the angle in problem 3 into an angle of 60°.

   b.

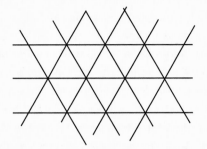

Hints and Comments

Materials

straightedge (one per group of students);
rectangular transparency strip, 2 centimeters wide (one per group of students);
rectangular transparency strips, 3 centimeters wide (two per group of students);
drawing paper (one sheet per group of students)

Overview

Students use transparency strips to construct parallelograms. Then they look for characteristics of a parallelogram.

About the Mathematics

On this page, a parallelogram is presented as a special quadrilateral with parallel sides.

Planning

Students may work on this activity in small groups. The activity is continued on the next page.

Comments About the Solutions

Activity

Note that the only real requirement for the strips is that they have parallel edges. Parallelograms can also be constructed with two rectangular strips of paper; however, strips of transparencies make it easier to visualize the parallelogram.

Notes

iv When students draw the set of parallelograms, be sure they know that a rectangle is a special parallelogram.

6 Groups could put their summaries on a poster with examples of various parallelograms.

Some students may find pairs of parallel lines either by looking at them or by actually measuring them.

7 Students cannot use the transparency strips from the activity because those strips are not the correct width.

5. Using its name, *parallelogram,* describe the properties of the quadrilateral you formed.

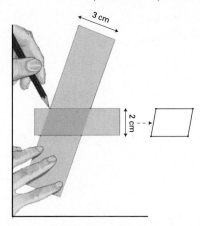

iii. Move the transparencies around to make different parallelograms.

iv. Use one strip of 2 cm and one strip of 3 cm to draw one set of parallelograms. The figure shows how to mark the vertices of the parallelogram. These vertices can be used to draw the sides of each parallelogram. Use your ruler as a straightedge.

v. Draw another set of parallelograms using two strips of 3 cm.

6. List some of the similarities and differences between each set of parallelograms.

Summarize your results. Include the following in your summary:

- general characteristics of parallelograms;
- how equilateral parallelograms differ from non-equilateral parallelograms;
- any other special names for parallelograms;
- how parallelograms differ from other quadrilaterals.

7. Decide whether each of these figures is a parallelogram. Justify your answer.

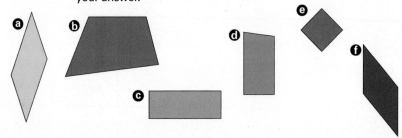

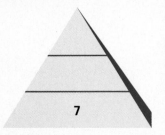

Assessment Pyramid

7

Recognize and classify quadrilaterals.

Reaching All Learners

Accommodation

For problem 6, you may want to have triangles, straightedges, or protractors available for students who want to check for parallel lines.

Vocabulary Building

On the previous page, a parallelogram is presented as a special quadrilateral with parallel sides. Students may remember names for special parallelograms, like *rhombus*. If not, on the next page, rectangles, rhombi, and squares are introduced as special parallelograms.

Solutions and Samples

Activity

5. Answers will vary. Sample responses:

The sides of each parallelogram made with the two 3-cm strips are always equal and are at least 3 cm long. (They are exactly 3 cm long if the parallelogram is a square.)

Each parallelogram made with one 2-cm strip and one 3-cm strip has two sides that are at least 2 cm long and two sides that are at least 3 cm long. (Some may be rectangles.)

All the parallelograms have opposite angles equal, opposite sides of equal length, and opposite sides parallel.

6. Summaries will vary. Sample responses:

A parallelogram has four sides. Opposite sides have the same length and are parallel. Also, opposite angles are equal.

Equilateral parallelograms have four equal sides, non-equilateral parallelograms have only two pairs of equal sides.

A special name for other parallelograms is, for example, a rectangle, a square, and a rhombus.

Other quadrilaterals, like the one shown below, may have four sides that are of different lengths that are not parallel, and four angles that are not equal.

7. Figures **a**, **c**, **e**, and **f** are parallelograms; **b** and **d** are not.

Students may justify their answers by measuring the opposite sides or the opposite angles of each parallelogram, by using a straightedge and triangle to check that opposite sides are parallel, or by making new strips that match the measurements of the parallelograms.

Hints and Comments

Materials

see previous page;
straightedge (optional, one per student);
plastic or cardboard triangle (optional, one per student)

Overview

Students make different parallelograms using their strips. Then they look for characteristics of a parallelogram.

About the Mathematics

Equal sets of opposite angles or equal sets of opposite sides are each sufficient criteria for identifying parallelograms.

Planning

Students continue the activity from the previous page in small groups. They can also work in small groups on problem 5.

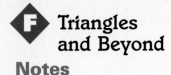
Triangles and Beyond **F**

Notes

Lula Red Cloud is a Lakota Sioux quilt maker from the Pine Ridge Reservation in South Dakota. She uses many patterns to make quilts. Here is a quilt she made for a ceremony. She used a star pattern for this design.

The vibrant colors she uses are meaningful in her art. In this quilt, the colors refer to the morning sun, the earth, and the sky.

A Tribute to the Invisible People Quilt, 1996, Lula Red Cloud (Sioux), Hermosa, Dakota. MSUM

8a If students have difficulties, you may give a hint to focus on the center point of the star.

The patches that make the star are congruent parallelograms.

8. **a.** Describe the side lengths of one parallelogram in this pattern.

   b. Without measuring, determine the size of each angle of one parallelogram.

Some parallelograms have special shapes and names.

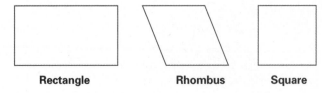

Rectangle   **Rhombus**   **Square**

9 Note: All of these figures are (special) parallelograms.

9. Describe the characteristics of each parallelogram.

10. Classify the parallelograms that you drew in the Parallelograms Activity on page 45.

Assessment Pyramid

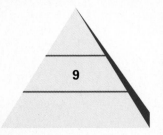

Describe geometric figures using words and diagrams.

Reaching All Learners

Intervention

A Venn diagram with examples of various kinds of parallelograms is helpful for many students to understand that a square fits in both the rectangle and rhombus category.

Vocabulary Building

For problem 9, add *rectangle*, *rhombus*, and *square* to your glossary. You also might want students to put these terms on index cards with the definition on the back of the card. Be sure they realize that a square is a special rectangle and a special rhombus.

Solutions and Samples

8. a. The sides are all equal.

   b. There are different strategies to find the size of the angles.

     Possible strategy: Around the center point of the star there are eight parallelograms.

So the two smallest angles of one parallelogram are 360° ÷ 8 = 45° each.

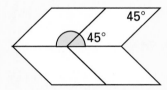

In another part of the pattern, you can see that the small 45° angle of a parallelogram and a large angle of the parallelogram form together an angle of 180°. So the two largest angles of the parallelogram are 180° − 45° = 135° each.

9. Answers will vary. Sample response:

A rectangle is a parallelogram with four equal angles that each measure 90°. Most rectangles have one pair of sides that is longer than the other pair.

A rhombus is a parallelogram with four equal sides, but not necessarily four equal angles.

A square is a parallelogram with four equal sides and four equal angles. A square can also be defined as a rectangle and a rhombus.

10. Answers will vary. Students may note that all parallelograms made with the pair of 3-cm strips are rhombuses or squares. None of those made with the 2-cm strip and the 3-cm strip together are rhombuses or squares, but some may be rectangles.

Hints and Comments

Overview

Students investigate parallelograms that are elements of a quilt. They determine the size of the angles. Then they list characteristics of a rectangle, a rhombus, and a square as being special parallelograms and classify parallelograms.

About the Mathematics

The eight congruent parallelograms that are in the center point of the pattern fill exactly the area around that point. This pattern could be made by starting with one parallelogram and rotating it seven times. Students will investigate this idea of making regular shapes when they construct polygons at the end of this section. But then they start with an isosceles triangle instead of a parallelogram.

Planning

Students may work individually or in small groups on problems 8–10. Problem 9 may be used as Informal Assessment. Discuss students' answers of problems 8 and 9 before they continue with problem 10.

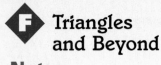
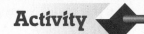
Combining Transformations

For this activity, you will combine a rotation and a translation.

You will need:

- scissors;
- thick paper;
- drawing paper;
- two colored pencils; and
- a pencil.

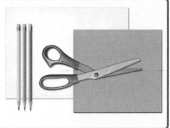

i You may want to assign some students to use an acute triangle, some a right triangle, and some an obtuse triangle for this activity. Then have them exchange triangles with another student for making the second parallelogram.

iii Ask students how they can be sure the angles that they made the same color are equal. They should discover that opposite angles of a parallelogram are equal.

i. Make a cutout of any triangle and trace it on a piece of paper.

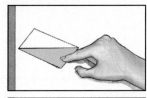

ii. Rotate the triangle 180° around one vertex until it is upside down.

iii. Translate the triangle so it aligns alongside or below the starting triangle and trace its final position.

- Describe the quadrilateral.

- Color the angles of your quadrilateral so angles of the same measure are the same color.

- Repeat steps **i** through **iii** with a different triangle.

- Summarize the activity.

Reaching All Learners

Act It Out

Before starting this activity is a good time to review the three transformations (translation, rotation, reflection). Students could demonstrate the movements with their bodies or with any object.

Extension

You may want to ask students, *Can you rotate a triangle around any vertex to make a parallelogram?* (Yes.) *Will the result always be the same after you have translated the triangle?* (No.) Encourage students to find the answers by making drawings.

Solutions and Samples

Activity

iii. • a parallelogram

- Ask students, *How can you be sure that the angles you chose are equal?* (Because they were made from the same triangle.)

- Figures will vary, depending on the triangle chosen. Sample responses:

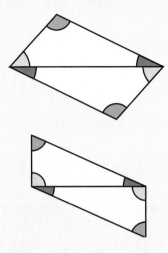

- Summaries will vary. Sample summary:

  When you have a triangle and trace it and then rotate it over 180° and translate it and trace it again, the result will always be a parallelogram. In this way you can see that opposite angles in a parallelogram are equal.

Hints and Comments

Materials

drawing paper (two sheets per student);
scissors (one pair per student);
colored pencils (one box per student);
ruler (one per student);
thick paper or index cards

Overview

Students rotate and then translate a triangle to make a parallelogram.

About the Mathematics

Two angles in a quadrilateral are either consecutive or opposite.

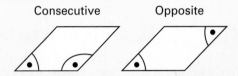

In a parallelogram, these angle pairs are special. From the previous activity (pages 45 and 46), students should understand that opposite angles of a parallelogram are equal. The transformation construction also shows that in a parallelogram, the sum of consecutive angles is 180°.

Planning

Students may work in small groups on this activity.

Comments About the Solutions

Activity

This activity is important for the development of students' understanding of parallelograms and their characteristics. Note: The results of students' investigations may help them see that a diagonal of a parallelogram divides two angles in two parts that are not necessarily equal.

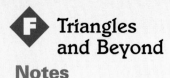 
F Triangles and Beyond

Notes

Activity

Make sure students understand the concept of the vertex angle. Then students start the activity, individually or in small groups.

Encourage students to use isosceles triangles with the vertex angle of various sizes. Then have students share their findings with the whole class. Be sure they know which angle is the vertex angle.

11. What can you rotate and translate to make a rhombus?

12. What type of triangle can you rotate and translate to make a rectangle?

Activity

Constructing Polygons

For this activity, you will need:

- thick paper;
- scissors; and
- drawing paper.

i. Draw an isosceles triangle and color the **vertex angle** (the angle that is formed by the two equal sides).

ii. Cut out the triangle and trace it on a sheet of paper.

iii. Rotate the triangle around the vertex, as shown.

iv. Trace the triangle and rotate it again.

v. Continue this process until you have eight copies.

- Did all eight copies fit together with no gaps or overlaps? Did any of your classmates'?

Assessment Pyramid

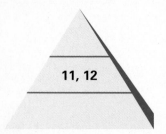

11, 12

Describe transformations using words and diagrams.

Reaching All Learners

Intervention

If a student cannot get started on problems 11 and 12, you might suggest they work backwards. You might also have them make a rhombus without right angles and one with right angles.

Solutions and Samples

11. an isosceles triangle:

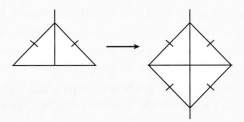

12. a right triangle:

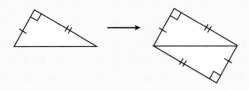

Notice that if you start with the first triangle and

rotate it, the translation should be at an angle rather than horizontal, as shown below.

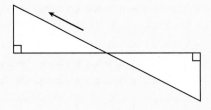

Activity

Answers will vary. The eight copies will not fit together unless the vertex angle of the isosceles triangle is 45°.

Hints and Comments

Materials

drawing paper (two sheets per student);
scissors (one pair per student);
compass card or protractor (one per student);
ruler (one per student);
pair of compasses (one per student)

Overview

Students find out what type of triangle can be used to make a rhombus or a rectangle when rotating and translating the triangle.

In a new activity students cut an isosceles triangle out of a piece of paper and rotate the triangle.

About the Mathematics

An isosceles triangle can be constructed in different ways. The constructions are based on the following topics.

- Section B: Use a pair of compasses.

- Section C: Choose a number of degrees for the base angles, for example 70°. Then use a compass card or protractor to construct these angles.

- Section E: Use symmetry.

  Fold a piece of paper and cut out a right triangle. Note that one of the legs of the right triangle has to coincide with the folding line.

Planning

Students can work individually on problems 11 and 12. These problems can be used as informal assessment or assigned as homework.

Introduce the activity in a class discussion. Ask students how they would construct an isosceles triangle.

F Triangles and Beyond

Notes

F Triangles and Beyond

George wanted to make an octagon (a polygon with eight angles and eight sides), but the isosceles triangle that he used did not work. His drawing turned out like the one below.

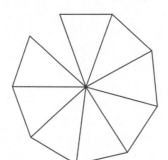

13a Allow students to use a variety of strategies to find the size of the vertex angle. Then you may want them to explain to one another how they found their solution.

13d Students may need the definition of *regular polygon* if they have not yet done the unit *Packages and Polygons*. Regular polygons have all sides the same length and all angles the same size.

13. **a.** Create a triangle that forms an octagon when you rotate and trace it eight times.

   b. How can you determine whether rotating and tracing a triangle will form an octagon?

   c. Create a triangle that forms a hexagon when you rotate and trace it six times.

   d. Is each of the polygons regular? Explain why or why not. Include in your explanation the definition of a regular polygon.

   e. Can every regular polygon be created by rotating and tracing an isosceles triangle? If so, explain the process. If not, explain why it cannot be done.

Sasha says, "To get a complete regular polygon, the size of the vertex angle will be exactly 360° divided by the number of sides."

14. **a.** Explain why Sasha's method works.

   b. When is the size of the vertex angle a factor of 360°?

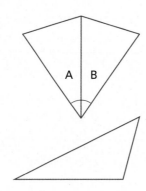

15. **a.** Describe two transformations that use isosceles triangle *A* to create triangle *B*.

   b. If you continue this pattern until you have a decagon (10-gon), does it matter which of the two transformations you use?

15c Make sure students choose a variety of triangles that are not isosceles to reflect and rotate. Then have them share their results with the class.

   c. Notice that triangle *A* is an isosceles triangle. Investigate whether the two transformations you selected produce the same result if the triangle is not isosceles. You might use this triangle. Summarize your results.

Assessment Pyramid

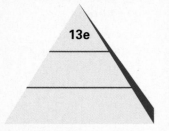

13e

Use counterexamples to justify geometric relationships.

Reaching All Learners

Extension

You may wish to have students make a regular quadrilateral, regular pentagon, regular hexagon, and regular octagon by rotating or reflecting an isosceles triangle and then drawing all the line of symmetry in each. Ask, *Is there a relationship between the number of lines of symmetry and the number of sides?*

You may want students to draw pictures of the reflections and rotations of the triangle described in problem 13c.

Solutions and Samples

13. a.

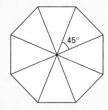

b. The vertex angle must be 360° ÷ 8 = 45°.

c.

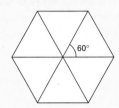

d. Yes. Explanations may vary. Sample explanation:

A polygon is regular when the angles have the same size and the sides have the same lengths.

e. Yes. Explanations may vary.

The following polygons can be made with isosceles triangles that have the indicated vertex angles.

Regular Polygon	Vertex Angle
Square	360° ÷ 4 = 90°
Pentagon	360° ÷ 5 = 72°
Hexagon	360° ÷ 6 = 60°
Nonagon	360° ÷ 9 = 40°
Decagon	360° ÷ 10 = 36°

Any regular polygon can be created from an isosceles triangle by determining the size of the vertex angle and then constructing the isosceles triangle accordingly.

14. a. If the vertex angle times the number of sides is equal to 360 degrees, all of the vertex angles together will complete a full turn.

b. The size of the vertex angle is a factor of 360 when the angle measure divides into 360 evenly. However, 180 and 360 divide into 360 evenly but are not possible as a vertex angle of a triangle.

15. a. A reflection or a rotation.

b. No.

Hints and Comments

Overview

Students find out what triangle, when rotated, can make an octagon and what triangle can make a hexagon. They investigate whether translation, rotation, or reflection can be used to make a 10-gon. Then they investigate whether or not they would get the same result if they started with a triangle that is not isosceles.

About the Mathematics

Students may remember the regular polygons from the unit *Packages and Polygons*. Any regular polygon can be divided into a number of congruent isosceles triangles. The measurement of the vertex angle of one such triangle can be found by dividing 360° by the number of triangles.

Comments About the Solutions

13. a. You may want students to explain to one another how they found their solutions. Some students may say that an octagon can be made from eight triangles; half the octagon has four triangles; and half of that has two triangles. The vertex angle of these two triangles together is 90°:

13. e. Students may answer with specific examples or may generalize with a high level of understanding. It is important that students see that this process is not limited to hexagons and octagons. If time permits, let students experiment with some other regular polygons.

15. c. Some students may find it easier to explain by using a drawing of what the movements would produce. If the starting triangle is not isosceles, a reflection over a side will change the orientation; a rotation will provide the same orientation but will not form a regular polygon.

c. If the starting triangle is not isosceles, the reflection will give a different result. A rotation also will give a different result. You will not end up with a regular polygon with either movement.

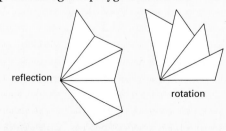

reflection

rotation

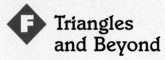
Notes

Fractals can be explored as an extension activity.

Math History

Fractals

A **fractal** is a geometric object that has self-similarity. This means that the structure of the object looks the same from very close or very far away. Fractals can be created by repeating a simple procedure over and over.

Many objects found in nature have some of the characteristics of fractals. This broccoli shows the self-similarity of a fractal.

A famous fractal is called the *Sierpiński Triangle*. This fractal, described by Waclaw Sierpiński in 1915, appears in Italian art from the 13th century. The fractal is made entirely of triangles.

1. To make a Sierpiński Triangle, start with a solid triangle.

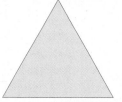

2. Find the midpoint of each side. Connect the midpoints to form four congruent triangles inside of the original triangle. Cut out the center triangle. This is one iteration.

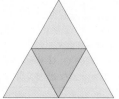

3. Do step 2 to each of the colored triangles.

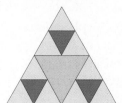

4. Step 2 can be repeated over and over. The Sierpiński Triangle can be used to make beautiful designs.

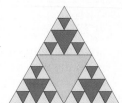

Reaching All Learners

Advanced Learners

Have students find examples of other fractals in library books or on the Internet. Encourage students to explain how to create fractals that start with other figures.

Hints and Comments

Overview

This can be completed by students for additional credit or assigned as an Extension activity.

Notes

This would be a good opportunity to have students review the properties learned so far in this unit.

Have students reread the section summaries as part of their review for the unit assessment.

Also review the definition of rectangle, rhombus, and square.

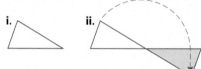 **Summary**

A **parallelogram** is a four-sided figure formed by the intersection of two pairs of parallel lines. **Rectangles**, **rhombuses**, and **squares** are special kinds of parallelograms.

By combining a rotation and a translation, you can use any triangle to draw a parallelogram.

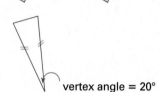

i. ii. iii.

A rotation and a reflection sometimes produce the same result.

For example, begin with an isosceles triangle with a **vertex angle** of 20°.

vertex angle = 20°

A rotation of 20° around the vertex angle gives the same result as a reflection over one of the equal sides.

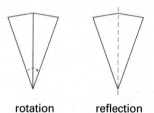

rotation   reflection

Regular polygons can be made by rotating isosceles triangles. The measure of the vertex angle of an isosceles triangle determines whether the triangle will form a regular polygon. The angle measure is 360° divided by the number of the triangles.

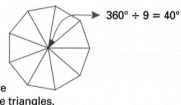

360° ÷ 9 = 40°

Reaching All Learners

Extension

You could ask students to find examples of regular polygons in the real world and bring in a sketch or photo of examples.

Hints and Comments

Overview

Students read the Summary, which reviews the main concepts covered in this section.

Planning

You may want to discuss this Summary in class. Ask students for:

- the criteria for a parallelogram being a rectangle, a rhombus, or a square;
- the properties of special triangles (isosceles, equilateral);
- the properties of regular polygons; and
- the meaning of the sentence, "The angle must be a *factor* of 360°."

Extension

For some students who are more visual learners, the following assignment can be very helpful to have an overview of all properties of special equilaterals.

Draw a parallelogram (rhombus, square). Use colors and/or symbols to indicate all properties.

(Arrows can be used to indicate parallel sides.)

Sample solution:

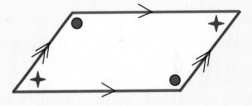

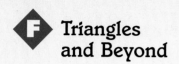

Triangles and Beyond

Check Your Work

1. Describe how you can determine if a shape is a parallelogram.

2. If a shape is a parallelogram, how can you tell if it is a

   a. rectangle?   **b.** rhombus?   **c.** square?

3. Study the two shapes. Describe several ways to determine whether each of the following statements applies:

   a. Each shape is a parallelogram.

   b. The two shapes are congruent.

Figure A

Figure B

4. **a.** On **Student Activity Sheet 8**, draw a triangle in each regular polygon that can be rotated to create the polygon.

b. Find the measure of the vertex angle for each triangle.

For Further Reflection

As you travel home from school, make a list of the geometric figures you see that have at least one line of symmetry. Sketch at least three of these and bring them to class to share and discuss.

Assessment Pyramid

1, 2, 3, 4, ☐ FFR

Assesses Section F Goals

Reaching All Learners

Extension

Students could create a picture of an animal, using all six kinds of triangles (acute, right, obtuse, isosceles, equilateral, scalene) and identify the kinds by labeling them. Another option is to allow students to use a parallelogram or allow them to use transformations and identify them.

Solutions and Samples

Answers to Check Your Work

1. Here is one possible description:

    A shape is a parallelogram if it is a quadrilateral and its opposite sides are parallel. So to make sure both pairs of opposite sides are parallel, I can measure the distance between each pair at many different spots.

2. **a.** A rectangle has four right angles.

    b. A rhombus has four equal sides.

    c. A square has both four right angles and four equal sides.

3. **a.** Here are some possible ways to show that the shapes are parallelograms.

    I would see if both pairs of opposite sides are parallel.

    I would divide the quadrilateral into two triangles. Then I would see whether or not one triangle can be moved by a rotation and a translation so that it fits on the other triangle.

    I would measure the angles and compare them. If the opposite angles are equal, then it is a parallelogram.

    I would measure the sides. If both pairs of opposite sides are equal, then it is a parallelogram.

    b. Here are some possible ways to show that the shapes are congruent:

    I would measure the sides and the angles. If they match, then the shapes are congruent.

    I would cut out one shape and see whether or not it fits on the other. I would describe a transformation that would accomplish this same result.

4. **a.**

    b. Figure 1: 360° ÷ 8 = 45°

    Figure 2: 360° ÷ 6 = 60°

    Figure 3: 360° ÷ 6 = 60° for triangles in a hexagon

    360° ÷ 5 = 72° for triangles in a pentagon

Hints and Comments

Materials

Student Activity Sheet 8 (one per student)

Check Your Work Problems

These problems are designed for student self-assessment. A student who can answer the questions correctly has understood enough of the concepts taught in the section to complete problems addressing similar content on the unit assessment. Students who have difficulties in answering the questions without help may need extra practice.

This section is also useful for parents who want to help their children with their work.

Answers are provided in the student book. Have students discuss their answers with classmates.

After students complete Section F, you may assign appropriate activities from the Additional Practice section, located on page 58 and 59 of the *Triangles and Beyond* Student Book, for homework.

For Further Reflection

Answers depend on student observation and will vary. You may want to have students identify the line of symmetry for the figures they sketch.

Additional Practice

Section Ⓐ Triangles and Parallel Lines

1. Rodney arranged nine toothpicks to make three triangles. Without adding more toothpicks, show how he can rearrange this structure to make five triangles by moving only three toothpicks.

2. **a.** Draw a small triangle in the middle of a piece of paper.

   Suppose this triangle is one of a triangular pattern made by three families of parallel lines.

   b. Use your triangle to construct three families of parallel lines to show your triangular pattern.

3. **a.** On **Student Activity Sheet 9**, use different colors to outline each of the three triangles in the picture.

   b. In how many ways can the three triangles be stacked? Color the figures on **Student Activity Sheet 9** to show all the possibilities. You may not need all of the figures.

Section Ⓑ The Sides

1. In your notebook, draw an angle of 100°. Use this drawing to make a triangle in which the largest angle is 100° and the longest side is 5 cm. Label all three sides and angles in your drawing.

2. Is it possible to draw a triangle in which the largest angle is 80° and the longest side is 5 cm? If so, draw this triangle in your notebook and label all three sides and angles. If not, explain why.

3. Without making a drawing, determine whether it is possible to draw a triangle in which the largest angle is 50° and the longest side is 5 cm. Explain your answer.

Section A. Triangles and Parallel Lines

1. Drawings may vary. Sample drawing:

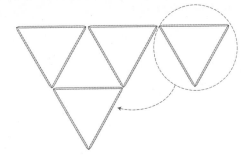

2. a. If a student doesn't know how to get started, you may give the hint to extend the sides of the triangle.

b.

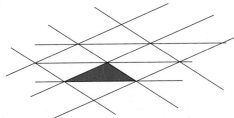

3. There are six possibilities. They are outlined in the following pictures.

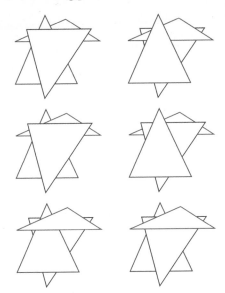

Section B. The Sides

1. Drawings and triangles will vary. Sample drawing:

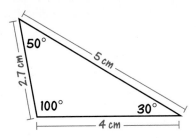

2. Yes, it is possible. Sample drawing:

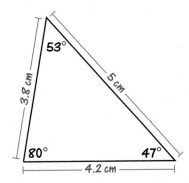

Students who answer, "No, it is not possible," may have tried to make one of the other sides too long, or one of the other angles larger than 80°.

3. It is not possible to draw a triangle in which the largest angle is 50° and the longest side is 5 cm. If one angle is 50°, then the other two angles must add to 130°, because 180° − 50° = 130°.

Since the two remaining angles must add to 130°, then at least one of the two remaining angles must be greater than 50° because 130° ÷ 2 = 65°. Therefore, the largest angle in a triangle can never be as small as 50°.

Puzzle Proof of the Pythagorean Theorem

These figures show two identical squares partitioned in two ways.

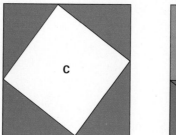

Figure 1

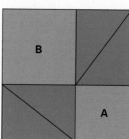

Figure 2

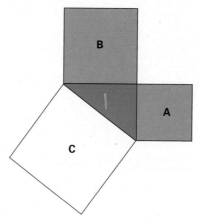

4. Using these pictures, explain why the white square in figure 1 has the same area as the sum of the blue squares in figure 2.

Section ◆ C Angles and Triangles

1. In your notebook, copy this picture and fill in the value of the missing angles. (Note: The drawing is not to scale.)

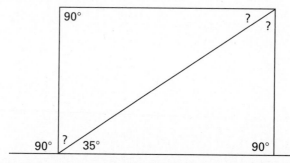

Section B. The Sides (continued)

4. In Figure 1, you see four congruent triangles and a large white square. In Figure 2, you see the same four triangles, but now the rest of the figure is divided in two blue squares. Therefore the white part in Figure 1 has the same area as the blue part in Figure 2.

Section C. Angles and Triangles

1.

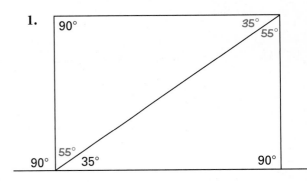

Additional Practice

2. Using a straightedge, draw a triangle in your notebook. Measure the three angles of your triangle with a compass card or protractor and label the angles. How can you tell that you measured the angles accurately?

3. This truck is moving down a ramp into a tunnel. Use **Student Activity Sheet 10** to locate the point at which the truck will be completely hidden from view by the wall. Show how you located this point.

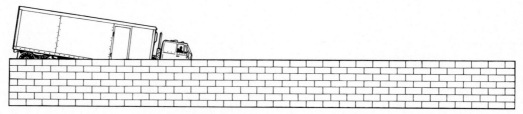

Section **D** Sides and Angles

For their math homework, Julia and Edgar have to determine which tree is closer to tree C: tree A or tree B. Unfortunately, tree C is across a stream from tree A and tree B.

1. **a.** Can you tell from the drawing which tree is closer to tree C?

   b. How can they determine which tree is closer?

Section C. Angles and Triangles (continued)

2. Drawings will vary. Sample drawing:

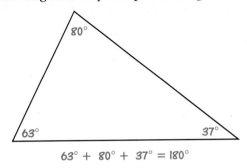

$$63° + 80° + 37° = 180°$$

The angles were measured correctly if the sum of the angles equals 180°.

3. Students should draw a line from the top of the truck to the ramp wall as shown below. The truck will be hidden from view at the point where the line touches the wall.

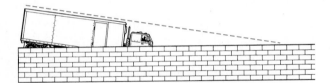

The assumption is that the road continues at the same level of steepness. The road is parallel to the roofline of the truck drawn.

Section D. Sides and Angles

1. **a.** You cannot tell which tree is closer from looking at the drawing. The two trees appear to be about the same distance from the third tree. In addition, it is possible that one tree is bigger than another but appears the same size because it is farther away.

   b. Answers will vary. Students may suggest that they measure the distances with string.

Julia and Edgar do not want to cross the stream to find out which tree is closer to tree C.

Instead, Julia uses two meter sticks and a sheet of cardboard for tree A. She makes an angle with the sticks, carefully aligning one stick with tree B and the other with tree C. She uses her cardboard and labels the angle vertex *A*.

Edgar uses two meter sticks and a sheet of cardboard for tree B. He makes an angle with his two meter sticks, aligning them with trees A and C. He uses his cardboard to record the angle and labels it angle *B*.

When Julia and Edgar compare their angles, they find that angle A is larger than angle B. Now they know which tree is closer to tree C.

2. Which tree do you think Julia and Edgar determine is closer to tree C? Why?

3. How did Julia and Edgar decide which tree is closer to tree C?

Section D. Sides and Angles (continued)

2. Tree A is closer to tree C.

Explanations will vary. Some students may try drawing different triangles to explore the relationship between the size of the angles and the length of the sides.

Since $\angle A$ is larger than $\angle B$, the distance from Tree B to Tree C is greater than the distance from Tree A to Tree C.

3. They used the relationship between the three angles and their opposite sides. Because $\angle A$ is larger than $\angle B$, BC is longer than AC.

Additional Practice

Section E Congruent Triangles

Suppose you want to make a triangle that will form a regular 20-gon when it is rotated and traced.

1. a. What is the measure of this triangle's vertex angle? Explain how you found your answer.

   b. Use your answer from part **a** to find the measure of one inside angle of a 20-gon. Explain your answer.

For this problem, you need four tiles like the one on the right.

2. Make a square using four of these tiles so the pattern in the square has each of the following:

   a. only one line of symmetry

   b. two lines of symmetry

   c. no lines of symmetry

Section F Triangles and Beyond

1. Joyce traces this parallelogram and cuts it out.

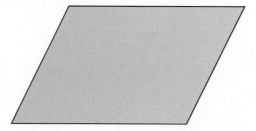

   a. Joyce says she can fold her parallelogram in half so that the two parts fit together exactly. Do you agree? Explain.

   b. Are there any types of parallelograms that can be folded together in half so that the two parts fit together exactly? Explain.

Section E. Congruent Triangles

1. a. The vertex angle of the isosceles triangle measures 18° (360° ÷ 20 = 18°).

b. One inside angle of a 20-gon measures 162°. Since the three angles of a triangle total 180°, and since the vertex angle measures 18°, the remaining two angles total 180° − 18° = 162°. In an isosceles triangle, the remaining two angles are equal, and 162° divided by two is 81° per angle. Recall that the regular 20-gon was made by rotating the isosceles triangle. So the inside angle of the 20-gon is made up of these two remaining angles, which is 81° + 81° = 162°. See the sample drawing:

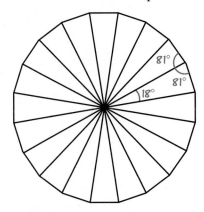

2. Different solutions are possible. Sample solutions:

a.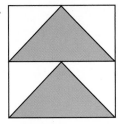

b.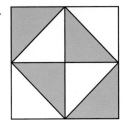

c.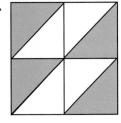

Section F. Triangles and Beyond

1. a. No. Joyce cannot fold her parallelogram in half so that the two parts fit together exactly because the parallelogram does not contain a line of reflection. So it does not have line symmetry.

b. Yes. Any rectangle, rhombus, or square can be folded in half so that its two parts fit together exactly.

They all contain a line of reflection and have line symmetry.

2. Parallelograms A and B are congruent.

a. In your notebook, trace parallelograms A and B. Show how to fit parallelogram A directly on top of parallelogram B using one or more of these transformations: translation, rotation, and reflection.

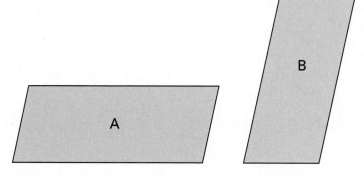

b. Is there more than one possible solution? Explain.

c. Which transformation (translation, rotation, or reflection) is required for all possible solutions?

Section F. Triangles and Beyond (continued)

2. a. Drawings will vary. The sample drawing shown below illustrates a translation followed by a reflection:

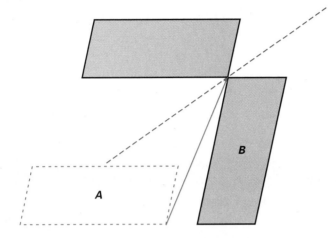

b. Yes. There are various solutions to part **a** because several movements of one type can have the same effect as one movement of another type. For example, several reflections may have the same result as rotating the original shape. Moreover, the sequence of movements can vary. For example, the above drawing could have been made by first using a reflection and then a translation.

c. A reflection is required for all possible solutions to part **a**.

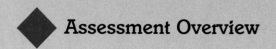

Assessment Overview

Unit assessments in *Mathematics in Context* include two quizzes and an unit test. Quiz 1 is to be used any time after students have completed Section C. Quiz 2 can be used after students have completed Section E. The Unit Test addresses most of the major goals of the unit. You can evaluate student responses to these assessments to determine what each student knows about the content goals addressed in this unit.

Pacing

Each Quiz is designed to take approximately 25 minutes to complete. The Unit Test was designed to be completed during a 45-minute class period. For more information on how to use these assessments, see the Planning Assessment section on the next page.

Goal	Assessment Opportunities		Problem Levels
• Use properties of triangles (e.g., sum of angles, side relationships, the Hinge theorem, and the Pythagorean theorem).	Quiz 1 Quiz 2 Test	Problem 3b Problem 2 Problems 1cd, 4, 5acd	
• Construct a triangle given side lengths.	Quiz 1 Quiz 2	Problem 2 Problem 1	
• Construct and identify (families of) parallel lines.	Quiz 1 Test	Problems 1ab Problem 3a	Level I
• Recognize and classify triangles.	Quiz 1 Quiz 2 Test	Problem 3a Problem 1 Problems 2, 3b, 5d	
• Recognize and classify quadrilaterals.	Test	Problem 3a	
• Understand and identify line symmetry	Quiz 2	Problems 3abc	
• Describe geometric figures using words and diagrams.	Test	Problem 3a	
• Describe transformations (translation, rotation, and reflection) using words and diagrams.	Quiz 2 Test	Problems 3bc Problems 1ab	Level II
• Use a compass to demonstrate and solve problems.	Quiz 1	Problem 2	
• Develop general statements for geometric relationships.	Test	Problem 5b	Level III

About the Mathematics

These assessment activities assess the major goals of ther *Triangles and Beyond* unit. Refer to the Goals and Assessment Opportunities section on the previous page for information regarding the goals that are assessed in each problem. Some of the problems that involve multiple skills and processes address more than one unit goal. To assess students' ability to engage in non-routine problem solving (a Level III goal in the Assessment Pyramid), some problems assess students' ability to use their skills and conceptual knowledge in new situations.

Planning Assessment

These assessments are designed for individual assessment; however, some problems can be done in pairs or small groups. It is important that students work individually if you want to evaluate each student's understanding and abilities.

Make sure you allow enough time for students to complete the problems. If students need more than one class session to complete the problems, it is suggested that they finish during the next mathematics class or you may assign select problems as a take-home activity. Students should be free to solve the problems their own way. Calculators may be used on the quizzes or unit test if students choose to use them.

If individual students have difficulties with any particular problems, you may give the student the option of making a second attempt after providing him or her a hint. You may also decide to use one of the optional problems or Extension activities not previously done in class as additional assessments for students who need more help.

Scoring

Solution and scoring guides are included for each quiz and the unit test. The method of scoring depends on the types of questions on each assessment. A holistic scoring approach could also be used to evaluate an entire quiz.

Several problems require students to explain their reasoning or justify their answers. For these questions, the reasoning used by students in solving the problems as well as the correctness of the answers should be considered in your scoring and grading scheme.

Student progress toward goals of the unit should be considered when reviewing student work. Descriptive statements and specific feedback are often more informative to students than a total score or grade. You might choose to record descriptive statements of select aspects of student work as evidence of student progress toward specific goals of the unit that you have identified as essential.

Use additional paper as needed.

1. a. How many families of parallel lines do you recognize in the picture?

b. When two families of parallel lines intersect, they form angles. Describe and sketch the angles that are formed.

Karen has two different sets of uncooked, dry spaghetti.

2. For each set of spaghetti, explain whether or not it is possible for Karen to construct a triangle.

Set 1:

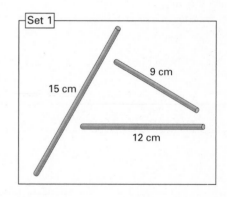

Set 1

15 cm

9 cm

12 cm

Set 2:

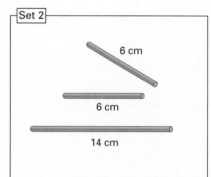

Set 2

6 cm

6 cm

14 cm

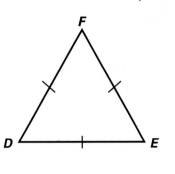

Four triangles are shown below. The slashes on the sides show which sides are of equal length.

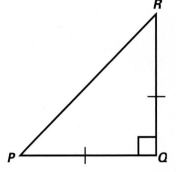

3. a. Classify each triangle by their sides (isosceles, equilateral, scalene) and their angles (acute, right, obtuse).

Triangle	Name (by sides)	Name (by angles)
ABC		
DEF		
KLM		
PQR		

b. Calculate the missing angles for each triangle without measuring them

(Note: The drawings are not to scale.) Show your work.

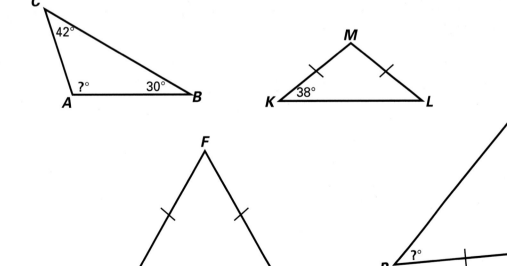

Use additional paper as needed.

The three squares on the right are used to make a triangle.

1. Will the triangle formed by these squares be acute, right, or obtuse? Explain your answer.

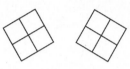

2. Calculate the missing side length for each of the following right triangles. Show your work.

A.

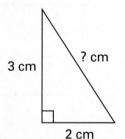

3 cm

? cm

2 cm

B.

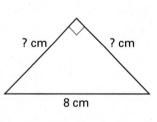

? cm   ? cm

8 cm

C.

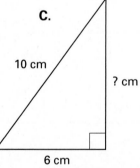

10 cm

? cm

6 cm

These figures have one or more lines of symmetry.

Figure 1

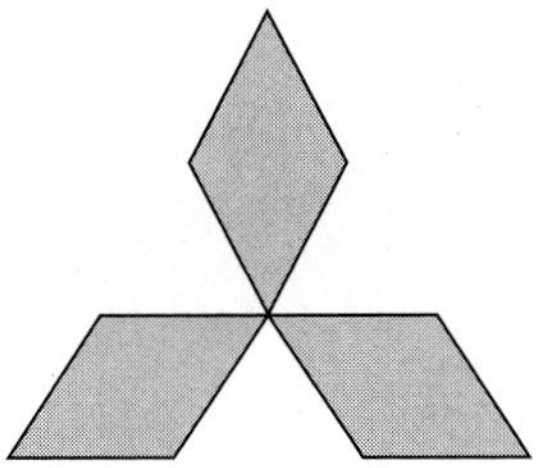

Figure 2

Figure 3

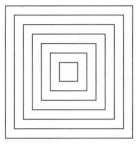

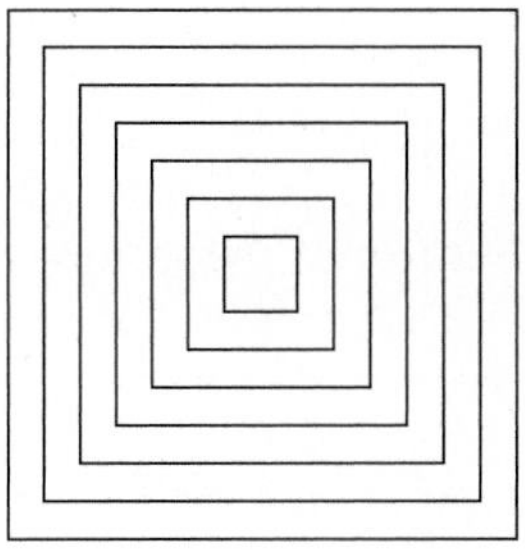

Figure 4

3. a. How many lines of symmetry does each figure have?

Figure 1:

Figure 2:

Figure 3:

Figure 4:

b. Which of these figures can be rotated over 180° so it fits on itself?

c. Figure 3 can be rotated over a different number of degrees so it fits on itself.

Write at least three different possible numbers of degrees.

Name _____   Date _____

Triangles and Beyond Unit Test

Use additional paper as needed.

All the triangles in the picture below are copies of triangle 1. They were made using rotation, translation, reflection, and a combination of these moves.

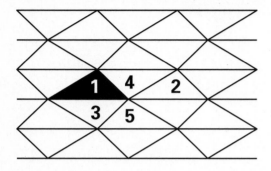

1. a. Describe how you could move triangle 1 to make copies 2, 3, 4, and 5.

1 → 2 : _____

1 → 3 : _____

1 → 4 : _____

1 → 5 : _____

b. Two of the angles in triangle 1 are 42° and 108°. What is the measure of the third angle in triangle 1?

c. What are the measures of the angles in triangle 2 and in triangle 4?

Triangle 2: _____

Triangle 4: _____

d. Triangles 1, 2, and 4 meet at a point where three angles touch. Describe the geometric property that is shown by where the three angles touch.

2. Tony has a set of three pieces of uncooked spaghetti. The lengths are 7 cm, 8 cm, and 10 cm. What type of triangle can he make with these pieces (without breaking them): a right, an obtuse, or an acute triangle? (Show or explain how you found your answer.)

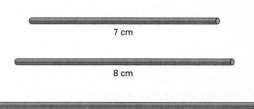

7 cm

8 cm

10 cm

3. a. What types of parallelograms can you find in this picture? Make a sketch of each type and describe the characteristics of each.

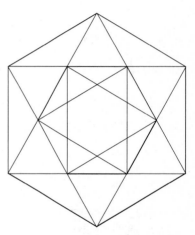

b. In the figure, find an example of . . .
- an equilateral triangle;
- an isosceles triangle;
- a scalene triangle.

Use additional paper as needed.

4. It is obvious that the dirt path that goes across the yard is shorter than the path along the sides of the rectangle.

If the shortest side of the rectangle is 100 m, and the longest side is 120 m, how much shorter is the dirt path? Show your work.

5. This is a picture of an equilateral triangle drawn inside a square.

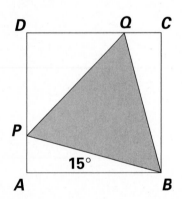

a. Calculate the measure of the angles of each triangle.

△ *PBQ*: _____ _____ _____

△ *PQD*: _____ _____ _____

△ *ABP*: _____ _____ _____

b. In the picture for problem 5a there are two small triangles
(△*PAB* and △*CQB*). Why are they congruent?

c. *PQ* = 10 cm
Calculate the side lengths of △*PQD*.

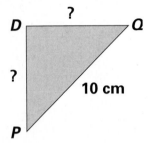

d. Calculate the height of equilateral △*PBQ*.

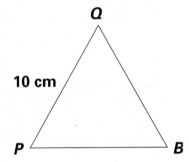

Triangles and Beyond Quiz 1
Solution and Scoring Guide

Possible student answer	Suggested number of score points	Problem level
1. a. There are 4 families. **b.** Possible angles are 45°, 90°, and 135°.	2 1 (describe) 1 (sketch)	I I
2. It is possible with Set 1 but not with Set 2. Set 1: 9 cm + 12 cm > 15 cm Set 2: 6 cm + 6 cm < 14 cm	3	I/II
3. a. | Triangle	Name (by sides)	Name (by angles)
ABC	scalene	obtuse
DEF	equilateral	acute
KLM	isosceles	obtuse
PQR	isosceles	right | **b.** $\angle B + \angle C = 42° + 30° = 72°$ $\angle A = 180° - 72° = 108°$ All angles are equal, so each is $180° \div 3 = 60°$. $\angle L = \angle K = 38°$ $\angle M = 180° - 38° - 38° = 104°$ $\angle P = \angle R$ and $\angle P + \angle R = 90°$ so $\angle P = \angle R = 90° \div 2 = 45°$	3 1 1 2 1	I I
Total score points	15	

Possible student answer	Suggested number of score points	Problem level
1. The area of the largest square is 9, and the other two together are 4 + 4 = 8. So it is not a right triangle. If the area of the largest square was 8, then it would be a right triangle, but the area is more, so the triangle is obtuse.	**1** (answer) **2** (explanation)	I
2. Triangle A: Triangle B: Triangle C:	2 2 2 2	I
3. a. Figure 1 has one, Figure 2 has three, Figure 3 has six, and Figure 4 has four lines of symmetry.	2	I
b. Figures 3 and 4	2	I/II
c. All possible numbers of degrees below 360° are: 30°, 60°, 90°, 120°, 150°, (180°), 210°, 240°, 270°, 300°, 330°	2	I/II
Total number of score points	15	

2. Triangle A:

Side length	Area
2	4
3	9
?	13

$? = \sqrt{13}\ (\approx 3.6)$

Triangle B:

Side length	Area
?	32
?	32
8	64

$? = \sqrt{32}\ (\approx 5.7)$

Triangle C:

Side length	Area
6	36
?	64
10	100

$? = \sqrt{64} = 8$

Triangles and Beyond Unit Test
Solution and Scoring Guide

Solutions	Score Points	Level
1. a. Answers will vary. Sample responses: Triangle 2 is a translation of triangle 1. Triangle 3 is a reflection of a triangle 1. Triangle 4 is a rotation and translation of triangle 1. Triangle 5 is a reflection, a rotation, and a translation of triangle 1 (a reflection and rotation, or a reflection and translation are also possible).	**4**	**II**
b. The third angle is 30°. Sample strategy: $42° + 108° = 150°$ $180° − 150° = 30°$ 30° 108° 42°	**1** (answer) **1** (strategy)	**II**
c. The angles are the same as the angles in triangle 1 (42°, 108°, and 30°).	**1**	**I**
d. The sum of the angles in a triangle is 180°. Together, the three angles form a straight line, which measures 180°.	**1**	**I**
2. It is an acute triangle. Sample strategies: Students can construct the triangle using a straightedge and a pair of compasses, and then measure the angles. Or they can compare the area of the squares on the sides: The two smallest squares have an area of $7 \times 7 = 49$ and $8 \times 8 = 64$. These two together have an area of 113. The largest square has an area of $10 \times 10 = 100$, so the triangle is not a right triangle because the largest square is too small. So the triangle is an acute triangle.	**1** (answer) **3** (strategy)	**I**
3. a. Sample characteristics: Rectangle: all angles are 90°, parallel sides are equal. Rhombus: all sides are equal, has two lines of symmetry.	**2** (drawings) **2** (characteristics)	**I/II**

Solutions	Score Points	Level

b.

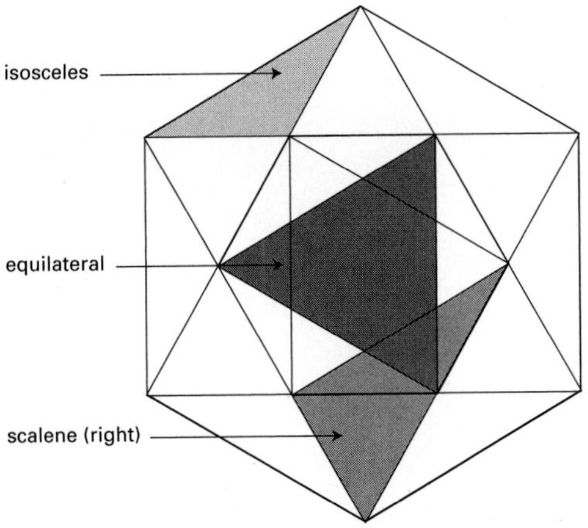
isosceles
equilateral
scalene (right)

Score Points: 3 — Level: I

---

4. The path along the sides is 100 + 120 = 220 m. (Score Points: 1 — Level: I)

The path that goes across: (Score Points: 3)

Side length	Area
100	10,000
120	14,400
?	24,400

$? = \sqrt{24{,}400} \approx 156.2$ m

So the difference is 220 − 156.2 = 63.8 m (Score Points: 1)

---

5. a. (Score Points: 3 — Level: I)

Triangle *PBQ* 180° ÷ 3 = 60° 60°, 60°, 60°
Triangle *PQD* 90° ÷ 2 = 45° 90°, 45°, 45°
Triangle *ABP* = triangle *BCQ*: 15°, 90°, 75°

b. The measure of the angles and the two side lengths are equal, so they fit on each other. (Score Points: 1 — Level: III)

c. (Score Points: 2 — Level: I)

Side length	Area
PD	50
QD	50
10	100

$PD = QD = \sqrt{50} \approx 7$ (Score Points: 2)

d. (Score Points: 4 extra points — Level: I)

Side length	Area
5	25
height	75
PQ = 10	100

height = $\sqrt{75} \approx 8.7$ cm

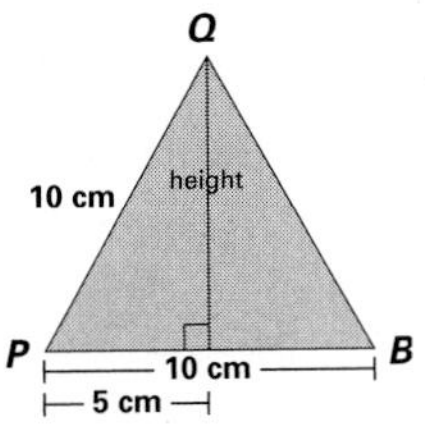
Q
10 cm
height
P
10 cm
B
5 cm

Total number of score points: 32 + 4

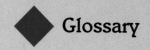

Glossary

The Glossary defines all vocabulary words indicated in this unit. It includes the mathematical terms that may be new to students, as well as words having to do with the contexts introduced in the unit. (Note: The Student Book has no glossary. This is in order to allow students to construct their own definitions, based on their personal experiences with the unit activities.)

The definitions below are specific to the use of the terms in this unit. The page numbers given are from the Student Book.

congruent figures (p. 36) figures that are copies of each other; figures with the same size and shape; figures that can fit on top of each other exactly

equilateral triangle (p. 9) a triangle with sides of equal length; a triangle with three equal angles

family of parallel lines (p. 4) a set of lines that are all parallel to each other

isosceles triangle (p. 9) a triangle with at least two sides of equal length; a triangle with at least two equal angles

line of reflection (p. 37) a line over which a figure is reflected, so that a copy of the figure appears on the other side of the line; the line that lies directly between two mirror images

line of symmetry (p. 39) a line such that if a figure is folded on it, then one half of the figure matches the other half

line symmetry (p. 39) the inclusion of a line of reflection

parallel (p. 4) extending in the same direction, staying the same distance apart and never intersecting

parallelogram (p. 45) a quadrilateral formed by the intersection of two pairs of parallel lines

quadrilateral (p. 45) a four-sided figure

reflection (p. 37) a mirror image; a copy of a figure made by flipping it over a line

regular polygon (p. 52) a polygon in which all sides are equal and all interior angles are equal.

rhombus (p. 49) a parallelogram with four equal sides

rotation (p. 37) a copy of a figure made by turning the figure around a particular point along a circular path

scalene triangle (p. 9) a triangle with three sides of different lengths

translation (p. 37) a copy of a figure made by sliding the figure so that every point on the figure moves the same distance in the same direction

vertex angle (p. 49) the angle that is formed by the two congruent sides of an isosceles triangle

Blackline Masters

Dear Family,

Your child will soon begin the *Mathematics in Context* geometry unit *Triangles and Beyond*. Below is a letter to your child that opens the unit, describing the unit and its goals.

At the beginning of this unit, students are asked to find examples of triangles. You may want to help your child find examples of triangles in architecture and art and in pictures in magazines and newspapers. After your child has worked through the unit, ask him or her to identify triangles by their sides (such as equilateral, isosceles, or scalene).

By the end of this unit, your child should be able to demonstrate how to identify the largest angle in a triangle simply by knowing the length of its sides.

As you walk through neighborhoods or drive through the countryside, have your child point out geometric shapes and properties. For example, your child should be able to show you a pair of parallel lines, such as two sidewalks running along opposite sides of the street or in rows of produce growing on a farm.

We hope you and your child enjoy studying geometry together!

Sincerely,

The Mathematics in Context Development Team

Dear Student,

Welcome to *Triangles and Beyond*.

Pythagoras, a famous mathematician, scientist, and philosopher, lived in Greece about 2,500 years ago. Pythagoras described a way of constructing right angles. In this unit, you will learn about the Pythagorean theorem and how you can use this theorem to find the length of sides of right triangles.

In this unit, there are many investigations of triangles and quadrilaterals and their special geometric properties.

You will study the properties of parallel lines and learn the differences between parallelograms, rectangles, rhombuses, and squares.

As you study this unit, look around you to see how the geometric shapes and properties you are studying appear in everyday objects. Does the shape of a picture change when you change its orientation on the wall from vertical to horizontal? How are parallel lines constructed? This unit will help you understand the properties of shapes of objects.

Sincerely,

The Mathematics in Context Development Team

Name _____

Student Activity Sheet 1
Use with *Triangles and Beyond,*
pages 4 and 5.

7. a. Select two parallel lines in the diagram and trace them using a colored pencil or marker.

  b. Measure how far apart the two lines are at several points. What do you notice?

  c. Measure the angles between the two lines and the road. What can you conclude?

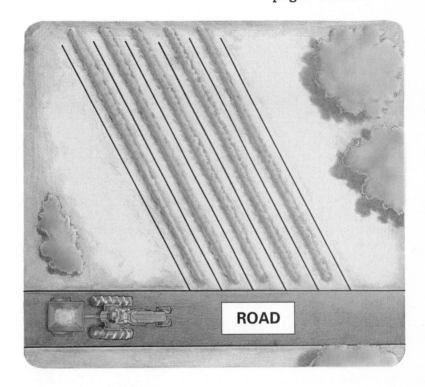

ROAD

9. a. Choose one triangular face. How many families of parallel lines can you find on that face?

  b. Highlight each family of parallel lines with a different color.

Name _____

Trees

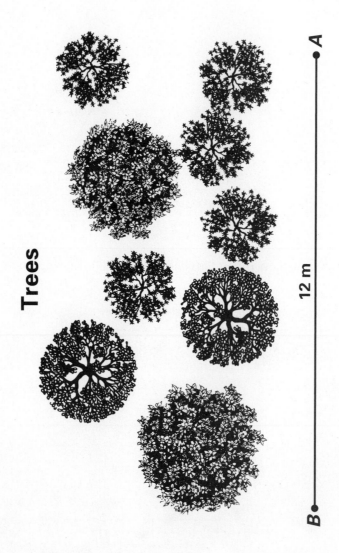

12 m

A

B

1. **a.** Use the symbols ● and ○ and **x** to mark all angles that have the same measure.

   b. Use your drawing to explain why the sum of the degrees of ● and ○ and **x** = 180°.

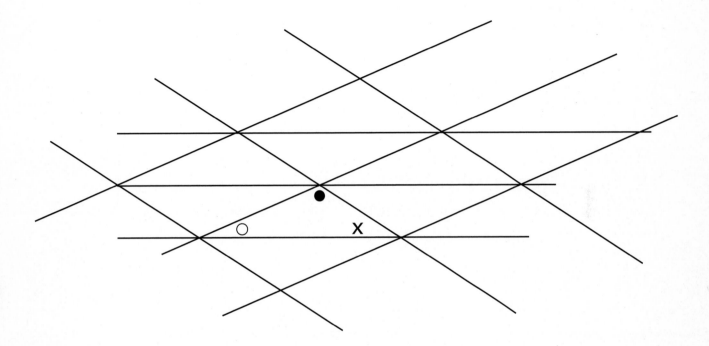

◆ **Student Activity Sheet 4**
Use with *Triangles and Beyond*, page 21.

Name _____

14. Fill in the values of the missing angles without measuring them.
(Note: The drawings are not to scale.)

a.
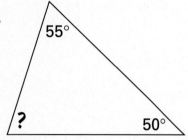

b.
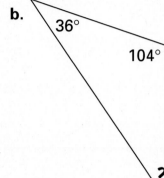

c.
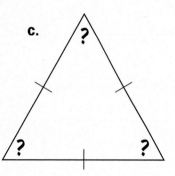

d.
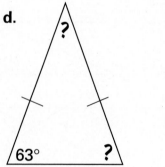

e.
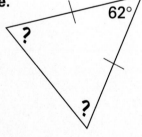

f.
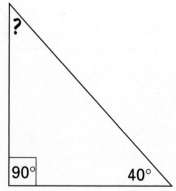

g.
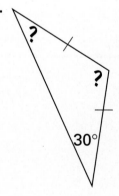

1. Fill in the value of the missing angles. The drawings are not to scale, so do not try to measure them to find the answers.

a.

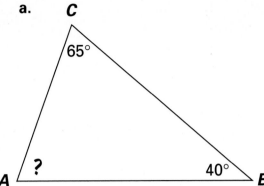

b.

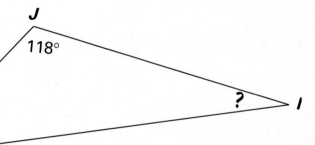

c.

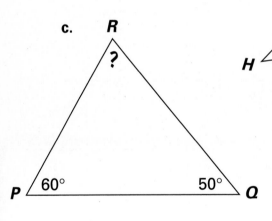

d.

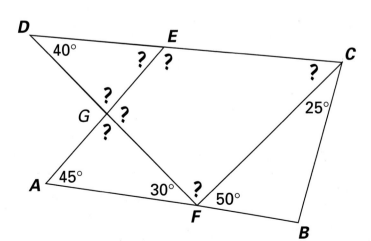

Student Activity Sheet 6

Use with *Triangles and Beyond*, page 25.

Name _____

Name _____

Use with *Triangles and Beyond*, page 25.

Name _____

4. a. Draw a triangle in each regular polygon that can be rotated to create the polygon.

 b. Find the measure of the vertex angle for each triangle.

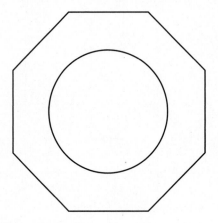

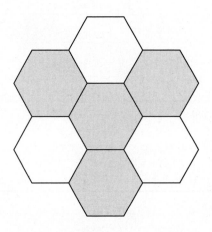

Name _____

Student Activity Sheet 9 ◆
Use with *Triangles and Beyond*, page 54.

3. a. Use different colors to outline each of the three triangles in the picture.

  b. In how many ways can the three triangles be stacked? Color the figures to show all the possibilities. You may not need all of the figures.

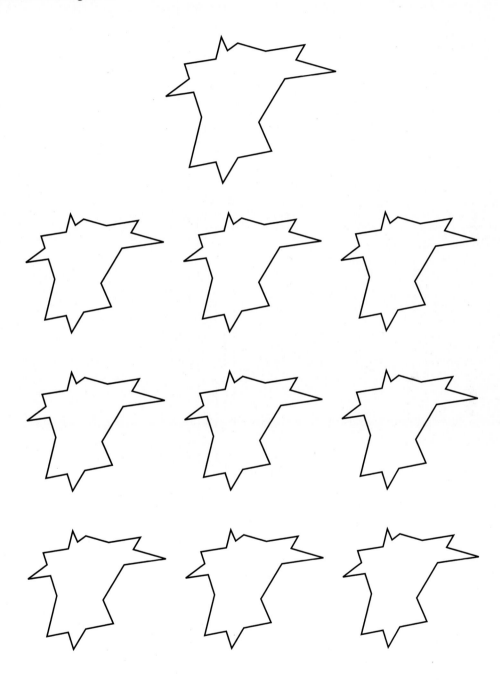

Name _____

3. This truck is moving down a ramp into a tunnel. Locate the point at which the truck will be completely hidden from view by the wall. Show how you located this point.

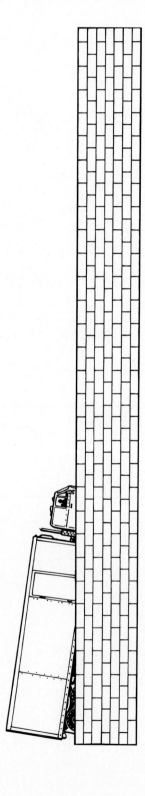